RAVING REFERRALS FOR DENTISTS

THE PROVEN STEP-BY-STEP SYSTEM TO ATTRACT PROFITABLE PATIENTS

BRANDON BARNUM

CHAIRMAN OF CHAMPIONDENTISTS.COM
CEO OF HOA.COM

JULIEANNE O'CONNOR

INFLUENCE COACH FOR DENTISTS

Raving Referrals for Dentists – The Proven Step-by-Step System to Attract Profitable Prospects

Paperback ISBN: 978-1-958405-68-0
Hardcover ISBN: 978-1-958405-56-7
eBook ISBN: 978-1-958405-57-4
Library of Congress Control Number: 2023901004

Publisher: The Champion Institute
Assisting Publisher: Spotlight Publishing House™
https://spotlightpublishinghouse.com
Main Editor: Becky Norwood
Interior Design: Marigold2k

Connect with Brandon Barnum Email: brandon@ravingreferrals.com
Web: www.BrandonBarnum.com
Web: www.RavingReferrals.com
LinkedIn: www.linkedin.com/in/brandonbarnum/

RAVING REFERRALS FOR DENTISTS

THE PROVEN STEP-BY-STEP SYSTEM TO ATTRACT PROFITABLE PATIENTS

BRANDON BARNUM

CHAIRMAN OF CHAMPIONDENTISTS.COM
CEO OF HOA.COM

JULIEANNE O'CONNOR

INFLUENCE COACH FOR DENTISTS

Goodyear, Arizona

Endorsements

for

Raving Referrals for Dentists

"If you want more income, influence, and impact, Brandon Barnum's new Raving Referrals book teaches what you need to succeed."

—Mark Victor Hansen
World's #1 best-selling non-fiction author
Chicken Soup for The Soul

"Buy this book now. You'll attract more referrals, win more business, and take it to the BANK!"

—Cheri Tree
CEO of Codebreaker Technologies

"This book gives you a practical and proven process to attract an endless stream of profitable prospects."

—Emmeline Saavedra
President of The Champions Institute

"When you incorporate the valuable information in this book, you'll find that you'll win more sales, do it in less time, and build a strong base of lifetime customers who will act as sources of raving referrals."

—Dr. Tony Alessandra
Author of The Platinum Rule for Sales
Mastery & Room Full of Referrals

"Raving Referrals delivers on what is needed to take dentistry to the next level while producing real results."

—Holland Haiis
Best-Selling Author of Consciously Connecting

"Nobody cares how much you know until they know how much you care. When they know you, like you, and trust you, they do lots of business with you. This is good for all involved."

—Duane Tinker
Dental Compliance Specialists

"Raving Referrals for Dentists is a must-read for both new and experienced dentists. It's clear, concise and will help you improve your referral process quickly and easily. It teaches you a proven process to grow both your revenue and valuation without adding unnecessary expense to your practice. Start building your tribe today using this book as your guide."

—Greg Essenmacher
Principal Dental Consultant at GnA Consult

"I have been building referral solutions in the dental industry for almost 20 years and our data shows that **88% of dentists report that referrals from current patients are their most successful marketing method**. Referrals work and this book gives you a proven process for attracting more patients quickly and predictably."

—Travis Rodgers, "The Referral Guy"
behind OneClick Referral

"I have been an oral & maxillofacial surgeon for over 50 years and built a successful practice on referrals using the principles outlined in the *Raving Referrals for Dentists* book. It is all about building relationships with colleagues and with your patients and this book shows you how to do that consistently.

—Dennis Smiler, DDS, MScD - Oral
& Maxillofacial Surgeon

Congratulations and thank you for getting this
Raving Referrals for Dentists book.

Scan the QR code below to view
a special video welcome message:

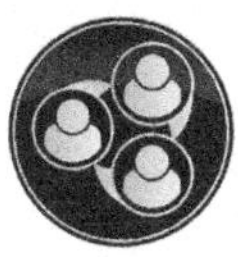

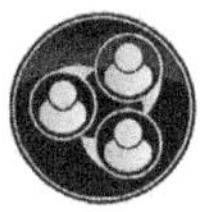

Foreword

In my two decades in the dental industry, I have attended many retirement parties, but one I went to last year stood out above them all.

The dentist's beautiful wife and kids stood next to him on stage all dressed up with big smiles of pride beaming from their faces. The room was packed with hundreds of former patients there to celebrate the dentist they all knew and loved. For decades, he had cared for their children and their grandchildren. His patients saw him as an extension of their family and of their community.

It was a touching ceremony and after the festivities wound down, I pulled him aside and asked him one simple question, "What was the secret to your success?" His answer was simple, "I grew my practice 100% by referrals."

This story is not alone. After building referral solutions in the dental industry for almost 20 years, our data at OneClick Referral shows that 88% of dentists identify referrals from current patients as their #1 most successful marketing method. There's simply nothing better than having your patients leave your office saying, "I Luv My Dentist."

Great smiles change lives. Great smiles create love. Great dental practices grow by referrals.

Research confirms that referred patients are more profitable, more enjoyable, and refer you more often than those you attract through any other marketing method. Unfortunately, while 75% of people choose their dentist based on the recommendation of a friend, very few dentists have mastered the art and science of generating referrals.

That's because dentists often have no formal training in sales and feel reluctant to ask for referrals. This book will help shift your mindset from selling to serving. The truth is that nothing beats the trust you gain when someone recommends you to their friends, family, colleagues, and coworkers.

These are the patients who are always a joy to see when they came into your office. These are the patients that accept your treatment plans without question. These are the patients who share stories of the impact you have had on their lives. While you may never see them outside your office, they consider you a friend and recommend you whenever they can.

That's why this book is so important for increasing the profitability of your practice. This "***Raving Referrals for Dentists***" book and accompanying course gives you a proven blueprint for growing your practice by referrals. Consistently and predictably.

Follow the proven process outlined in this book and put your referrals from patients and colleagues on autopilot. It really is easy when you follow this proven plan.

Travis Rodgers – CEO of OneClick Referral

Mr. Rodgers was the first to build an electronic referral in the dental industry in 2003, now called OneClick Referral. He was the first to build an integrated and automated word-of-mouth referral system. He is widely known as, "The Referral Guy" in the dental industry.

Dedication

I dedicate my life to glorifying God every day in every way. We are all blessed to live in a world with unlimited possibilities, and God, our creator, wants to co-create with you. I invite you to turn to Him and ASK for everything you want in life. Spend time in gratitude and prayer ASKing God to guide your life journey. As you invite God in and shine His light through your life, you will experience miracles and magic that lead to a life well-lived.

While my life is dedicated to God, this book is dedicated to my wife, Marlo, without whom none of my success would be possible. Marlo, you have stood by my side, supporting my dreams and aspirations for 29 years. I have watched you grow, mature, and evolve into an incredible person I am proud to call my wife for life.

Special thanks to Michael Keeter for your encouragement that this be the first extension of the Raving Referrals book series. Your friendship over these past two decades means a lot to me and I'm grateful we have had the opportunity to build our lives and raise our families together. To Emmeline and Wil Saavedra and the entire Champions Institute team for your support and partnership. I am beyond grateful to have you all in my life and excited about the impact we will create through this book and our Champion Dentists program.

Brandon

This book is dedicated to Brandon Barnum, who invited me to work with him on this project for dentists.

Dr. Mike Czubiak and Steve Sperry for bringing me into the dental space so many years ago.

My incredible clients.

Michael Keeter, for your countless connections and committed and loyal friendship.

Jay.

My dedicated husband Mark who always stands by me no matter what.

My inspiring empathic daughter Lotus who shows me how to live boldly into who I am.

My spirited warrior daughter Briana who makes me so very proud.

Penelope who shows me how resilience and love make all things possible.

And to the many amazing dentists and dental professionals who have become some of my dearest friends.

Thank you to each of you who have shown me behind the curtain.

You make Raving Referrals real.

Julieanne

IMAGINE...

Have you ever wanted to make a more significant difference in the world?

Now don't just skip past this question. Take a moment to give it some thought.

What would you do if your practice(s) was so successful that you suddenly found yourself with all the fortune and fame you've always dreamed of?

What if you had flocks of perfect patients flooding to your practice because of your stellar reputation and superb service?

What if you were able to leverage your expertise and respected authority in your field?

What if other businesses paid you to travel the world sharing your knowledge and wisdom within the industry?

How would you use your newfound influence and affluence? Would you simply retire and live out your days on some golf course or sunny beach? Or would you use your wealth and wisdom for good?

WE'RE ON A MISSION

We're asking you these questions because we're on a mission to impact and empower every person on the planet.

You see, we believe that every man, woman, and child deserve nutritious food, clean water, exceptional health care, empowering education, and opportunities for financial freedom.

Now, you may think the possibility of achieving that goal is entirely unrealistic, and you may be right. But the one thing we know is that every time we share our purpose and vision with others, we experience a deep sense of fulfillment and satisfaction. And we're willing to bet you feel that same indescribable joy every time you make a meaningful difference in the lives of others.

As you read this book, mastering the strategies that unlock all the income and influence you desire and deserve, we hope that you will, in turn, positively impact and uplift your team, associates, patients, vendors, and referral partners as well as your friends, family, neighbors, and community.

Together, we can make a difference and change the world in meaningful ways.

Brandon & Julieanne

Contents

Preface

CONGRATULATIONS!

For Investing in Yourself and Your Practice
For Pursuing a Faster Path to Success
For Discovering the System to Raving Referrals

Whether you are a general practitioner, pediatric dentist, endodontist, orthodontist, periodontist, prosthodontist or oral and maxillofacial surgeon, this book has been designed to help you attract more business for your practice, so you achieve the financial success you desire and deserve.

Since you're reading this book, we know a few things about you...

1. You are a highly trained dental professional with deep knowledge in anatomy and healthcare who likely has not been educated on marketing, sales or other business building strategies and techniques.
2. Your practice may not be quite where you want it to be. You simply aren't getting the kind of leads, referrals, prospects, and patients you need to earn the income you want.
3. Most likely, you are skilled at providing your service and just need a better system when it comes to marketing and business development.
4. Perhaps you feel awkward and uncomfortable asking for referrals, so you don't receive them as consistently as you'd like.
5. You already know some of the principles and practices in this book. Still, you don't have a formalized referral system

and sometimes rely on divine intervention, hoping new patient opportunities will appear each week.

6. Most importantly, you are serious about changing all that, and you're looking for a system that will generate a steady stream of highly qualified and profitable prospects.

You Are on The Right Path!

This book will empower you with time-tested, proven strategies, scripts, and secrets obtained from over two decades of researching, refining, and perfecting the referral process.

What we can give you goes far beyond simple theory. We've used these powerful principles and practices to build what we believe is the single most comprehensive and effective referral marketing system the world has ever known.

We are passionately committed to helping you transform your practice to create a consistent and dependable flow of *Raving Referrals* and profitable patients.

As Dr. Michael Hudson of Hudson Dental and Orthodontics in Gilbert, AZ says,

> *"Referrals are by far our #1 source of new patients. We spend $0 on marketing and get an average of 30 new patients each month, over 85% of which comes as referrals from our patients and referral partners."*

Our goal is that you start each week with a calendar that is full of new and/or profitable patient appointments, so you never have to worry about where your next referral is coming from. Imagine meeting with people every day who already trust you because they've been referred to by a loyal friend or professional that they have known for years.

I say "we" because WE IS THE KEY. This book is all about changing your mindset and approach when it comes to growing your practice.

Rather than being a lone wolf always out hunting for new opportunities by yourself, we want you to have a tribe of talented and trusted people you work with who are constantly helping refer patients back and forth so everyone wins together.

As you apply the Raving Referrals process, perfect prospects will flock to you, gift wrapped with trust, respect, and ready for the solutions and services you provide.

The Results Are In

Most business owners and professionals understand and agree that referrals are the best source of new business. After all, decades of research have proven this time and time again.

Empirical studies from major universities, publications, and research firms have concluded:

- People are 400% more likely to buy from you when they are referred.
- 90% of people trust recommendations from people they know.
- Referred patients are 16% more profitable than non-referred patients.
- 84% of Business-To-Business (B2B) sales start with a referral

According to Dr. Grayson Burgardt, owner of Periodontics and Implants of Peoria, AZ,

> *"Referrals drive our practice. 85% of all new patients come from 24 local dentists who refer us regularly. Our top referral partners send us 1-2 new cases per week and are truly our VIP partners."*

So, if referrals are so profitable, why do so many professionals struggle to develop a personal practice that generates new patient opportunities consistently?

What Holds You Back?

If you are like most of the dentists we serve, you may fall into one of the following categories:

- You are just too busy staying busy.
- You are new to dentistry and are just getting your business started.
- You don't seem to know the right people or have a strong enough network yet.
- You've never learned to build your practice by referral, and you aren't really sure how to start.

If any of these things have held you back in the past, you may feel like you grind away, day after day, with your team making tedious cold calls, buying bad leads, or throwing away good money on poorly performing marketing campaigns.

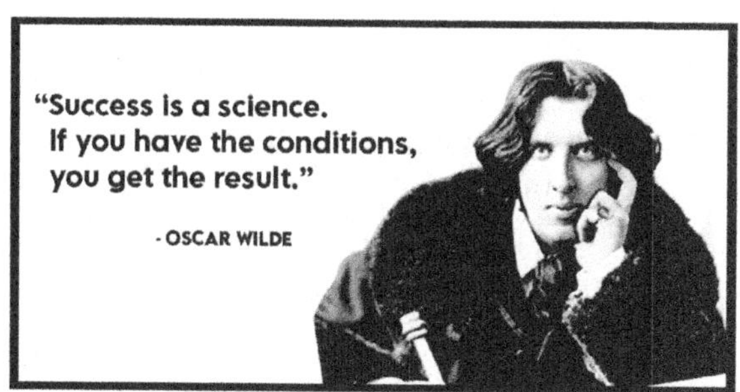

Perhaps you've been studying referrals for years and even belong to a study club, chamber of commerce, or popular dental association. You may already be getting some referrals and are looking to expand and improve the quantity and quality of the referrals you receive.

The good news is that if you simply follow the step-by-step process explained in this book, you can systematically build a strong referral business that will generate referrals for years to come.

Stop the Insanity

You've heard the definition of insanity is to do the same thing over and over and expect different results. Well, we want to commend you for investing in yourself and taking the time to learn these time-tested and proven tactics instead of doing what you've always done.

What we're going to teach you will be a total game-changer for you, your practice, and your family... but only if you take action and implement the simple steps outlined in this book.

After all, ACTION is the key to activating the law of attrACTION. If you follow this proven program and consistently take the quick and easy success steps, we will guide you through, your business and bank account will grow. As you expand your income, you'll unlock financial freedom and the time freedom you desire and deserve.

Our goal is to help you attract *Raving Referrals* quickly and consistently so you can spend more time doing what you love with the people you love. Whether pursuing your passions and hobbies, serving in your favorite charity or church, or traveling the world enjoying amazing experiences, everything you want can be achieved once you learn the secrets and the science of attracting *Raving Referrals*.

So that's our vision for you. But what's your goal?

How Much Money Do You Want to Make?

Ultimately, the number one reason you are reading this book is that you want to earn more money. If that's true for you, it's imperative that you set an attainable goal for exactly how much you want to earn over the next 12 months. You can then use your financial target as motivation to stay on track and take the actions needed to achieve your goal.

What is your Annual Income Goal for the next 12 months?

$____________________

What's Your WHY?

Now that you've declared how much money you want to earn in the next year, let's explore what really drives you. The following questions will help you gain clarity on your true reasons for achieving your Annual Income Goal.

1. Why is it important to you to increase your income and achieve your financial goal?

   ____

   ____

   ____

   ____

   ____

2. What would achieving your financial goal allow you to do that you can't do right now?

   ____

   ____

   ____

   ____

   ____

3. How will people benefit when you reach your goal?
   - Your Family (spouse, children, and grandchildren)
   - Your Friends
   - Your Company
   - Your Employees
   - Your Favorite Charities

   ____

   ____

   ____

   ____

   ____

4. How will your friends and family feel about you when you achieve your goal?

   ____
   ____
   ____
   ____
   ____

5. Beyond the money, how will you feel about yourself once you have achieved this level of financial success?

   ____
   ____
   ____
   ____
   ____

The reason it's so important to understand your *WHY* is that it is your *WHY* that really drives us as human beings. The clearer you are about *WHY* you want to achieve your desired outcome, the more driven and committed you will be to create those results.

Enlist Others in Your Success

To achieve success faster, share your goal with others who can help you reach it. This might include a business coach, partner, manager, employees, or even your referral partners. Ask them to hold you accountable or even partner on the program so they can build their business as you build yours.

After all, if you really want to lose weight, hiring a personal trainer committed to your success will dramatically increase your results. Just having a membership to the gym doesn't mean you actually show up and work out. Having a personal trainer that will hold you accountable ensures that when it comes to working out, you are doing what you should, when you should, exactly how you should. Granted, it takes time to see the results, but you will feel stronger, faster, and fitter over time. You'll see old fat transform into new muscle. You'll start to notice new lines and indentations on your stomach and problem areas where before there were only bulges and curves.

When it comes to building your business, the reality is you want as many people as possible invested in your success and cheering you on. The more champions you have for your business, the more business you will have.

From Success to Significance

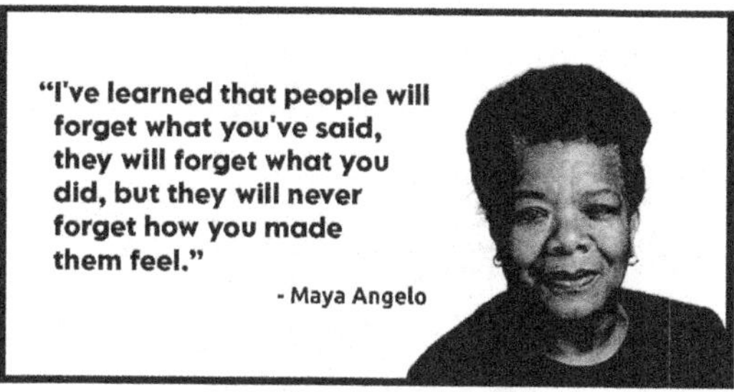

What's exciting to realize is that the success you create through-out your life and career can impact future generations if you do it right. Not just for you and your spouse. When you achieve serious success, you can leave a lasting legacy that changes the lives of you children, your grandchildren, and generations to come. Not to mention the impact you can have on your community and the causes you care about.

Our mission is to transform the lives of dentists around the world. That's why we are so committed to empowering and equipping you with the knowledge and tools that you need to succeed.

We want you to feel so confident and comfortable that you will take action immediately and that you'll consistently apply what we're going to teach you. If you do, you WILL get more referrals and patients, guaranteed!

We love what we do because we get to work with some of the best people and companies on the planet. There's nothing more rewarding than hearing stories of dentists worldwide who have gained financial freedom as a result of our system.

Our request is that as you put these practices and principles to work in your business, you will share your wins and success stories with us at RavingReferrals.com/success. We'd love nothing more than to spotlight your victories with our growing global community of people who are living a life powered by *Raving Referrals.*

Ready for us to show you the money? Scan the QR code below or use this link for a quick video message from Brandon Barnum:

https://ravingreferrals.com/money

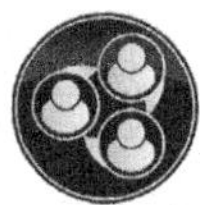

Introduction

Getting Personal

Over the past 27 years, I have been blessed to be mentored by some of the world's most influential and affluent people.

My career and professional travels have led me around the world to exciting locations, including Hong Kong, Macau, and Beijing, China; London, England; Zurich, Switzerland; Rome, Italy; Athens, Greece; Bogotá, Colombia; Caracas, Venezuela; Freetown, Sierra Leone; and Accra, Ghana.

I've hiked the Great Wall of China, convened in the U.S. Supreme Court in Washington D.C., celebrated with the 2nd man to walk on the moon, and flew in a private plane over Angel Falls, the tallest waterfall in the world smack dab in the Amazon rainforest.

I've been involved in billions of dollars of transactions, met with CEOs of massive corporations including Prudential, Patron, Paul Mitchell, Blockbuster, and Bank of America. I've hired top executives to help build my brands and grow my businesses, including the former Chief Marketing Officer from Mastercard and the former CEO of Guerilla Marketing.

I've taught countless people around the world through seminars, conferences, and webinars and have been blessed to have some of the world's most amazing thought leaders teaching our students. Authors and luminaries like Mark Victor Hansen of *Chicken Soup for the Soul,* Jack Canfield of *The Success Principles,* Michael Beckwith from *The Secret*, John Gray of *Men Are from Mars, Women Are from Venus*, Brendon Burchard of *High Performing Habits*, Chris and Janet Attwood of *The Passion Test*, and visionary futurists including Barbara Marx Hubbard, Dr. Don Beck, Lynn Twist, and Dr. Jean Houston to name a few, have been faculty members teaching and training our clients and community.

I've raised and donated millions of dollars for great charities, both here and abroad. One of my favorite projects was helping design and execute a fundraising campaign for the Mineseeker Foundation, whose patrons included Richard Branson, Brad Pitt, Queen Noor of Jordan, and Nelson Mandella, all of whom banded together to eliminate landmines from the face of the planet.

I've met with African chiefs, operated a diamond mine on the Gold Coast of Africa, and produced the single largest training of teachers in the African nation of Liberia presided over by the President of Liberia herself.

I was even fortunate enough to meet my idol and personal hero – Bono, the lead singer of the band U2.

Needless to say, at the age of 52, I've lived a rich, exciting, and fulfilling life.

The reason I share all of this with you is not to impress you but to impress upon you that anything you dream, and desire is possible. Every single one of the incidents and relationships I mentioned came after an introduction or referral. Before I teach you how to attract all the patients, associates, and people you need to fulfill your purpose and passions, let me take you back to the beginning of my story.

Humble Beginnings

As a child from a divorced home in the 1970s, my hippy mom hopped from job to job, never caring much about money or financial stability. Her wanderlust led to constant moves, which meant I had to attend different schools each and every year from kindergarten through sixth grade.

In addition to constantly changing where we lived, my mom was also continually changing jobs and careers. She did everything from working as a mechanic for Southern Pacific Railroad, working retail for a thrift shop, selling insurance, and even operating a bakery before eventually selling real estate.

Money was tight, and I grew up with vivid memories of watching Mom buy groceries with government food stamps. Then I would go to school, where they were nice enough to give me tickets for free breakfast and free lunch every day to ensure I had food to eat and didn't go hungry.

As you might imagine, after living with so little growing up, my true hunger was for success, so I grew up eager to achieve wealth and prosperity as far back as I can remember.

My First Referral Experience

My first experience with referrals came back in 1985 when I signed up for the Columbia House record and tape club. I was so excited to get my first shipment of 13 cassette tapes, which arrived for the low cost of just one penny (plus shipping and handling, of course).

This was the 80's, so I had all the popular albums by bands like U2, The Jacksons, Duran Duran, Thompson Twins, Journey, and many more. What excited me most was their offer to send me four more cassette tapes for each person I signed up for the music membership.

I quickly got 12 other kids from my high school to pay their penny and sign up for the program. It wasn't long before 48 more albums arrived. For a poor teenager with little money, it felt like I had won the lottery! My friends marveled at my music collection, and I enjoyed having albums from obscure artists like Icicle Works and Flock of Seagulls. You've gotta love the 80's.

That experience taught me the power that generating referrals can have on a business. It was also the first example I'd seen of a Referral Rewards program. Since then, I've used that same strategy to personally generate over $500,000,000 in closed transactions by referral.

Single Dad Life

My professional career started a decade later. I was 25 years old, still fresh out of college, and working as the Marketing Director for a regional estate planning law firm.

Having recently been awarded custody of my 2-year-old son, Sebastian, I found myself as a young single dad faced with many new life challenges, the biggest being financial.

With outrageous daycare expenses piled on top of my mortgage, I soon found myself faced with too much month at the end of the money. Can you relate?

After bouncing mortgage checks multiple times, I knew I had to change my financial situation if I was ever going to provide for my son. After exploring various opportunities and industries, I decided to accept a mortgage loan officer position at a prominent Savings and Loan. That's where I first uncovered the art and science of attracting Raving Referrals.

Mentored to Millions

As I started my new job, I was desperate to build my book of business. I felt intimidated, having no experience, no network, and no clue how to get either one. Needless to say, those first few months were rough!

As fortune would have it, one of my state's top producing loan officers worked at the desk next to mine. Every day I studied by his side, soaking up everything I could learn from this top producer who earned hundreds of thousands of dollars each year.

What amazed me is that this man had absolutely no personality. In fact, the rest of the office would giggle as he answered his phone, stating his name with a droll monotone that sounded like it belonged to the teacher from *Ferris Bueller's Day Off*: "Anyone? Anyone?"

Despite his lack of charisma, this man's phone rang off the hook with new loan applications. He was earning tens of thousands of dollars in commissions each month working 9 am to 5 pm and was generating the level of income and success I was hungry for.

So, I watched and listened in awe, asking as many questions as possible to learn his secrets for attracting so much business. I *had* to know what he was doing that made him so super successful.

It turns out he had cracked the code on attracting referrals. Over the years, he had built relationships with top professionals in complementary industries who were already serving the clients he wanted to attract. These pros were happy to refer clients to him because he had earned their trust and respect.

As a result, he never had to spend a dime on marketing and rarely spent any time prospecting. He had all the clients he could comfortably manage and rarely had to leave his desk except to grab some coffee and collect his fat paychecks.

As I studied this man's business intensively, I interviewed other top-producing mortgage and real estate professionals because I was committed to learning how the top 10% consistently outperformed the bottom 90% by leaps and bounds.

Lessons from Top Producers

These top producers taught me how the super successful generate massive income consistently and almost effortlessly. I learned proven tips, scripts, and strategies that have opened doors I could never have entered on my own.

By consistently engaging complementary professionals, I built deep, meaningful, trust-filled relationships that gave me referrals which helped 10X my income from $20,000 to over $200,000 annually in just 18 months after entering the mortgage business.

Since that time, I've used this formula to build relationships with some of the world's most affluent and influential people who have graciously recommended me to their clients and colleagues.

Needless to say, referrals have changed my life and continue to drive my success now over twenty years later. It's been an amazing adventure so far, and I hope you'll join me on this ride.

Since those early days, I helped build the world's largest referral network with more than five million members in over 200 countries. Now, as Chairman and CEO of HOA.com, I spend my time training and empowering the next generation of professionals and small business owners to grow their businesses by referral: challenging and empowering them to do more, be more, earn more, and give more for the betterment of all.

My hope is that you too will master these keys to *Raving Referrals* and that they forever change your life. If you implement just one of these success steps each week, you can increase your referral business and attract all the income, impact, and influence you desire and deserve.

Julieanne's Intro

Much like Brandon, I too started from humble beginnings, having grown up poor on a contaminated Rocketdyne test site outside of Reno, NV. Having been told I could get cancer at a young age from what I had been exposed to on our toxic property, I set out on a mission to learn what led to a meaningful life.

At first, I asked everyone I met, the secret to a happy marriage, and later I began asking everyone what gave them any form of sustainable happiness. The lessons were simple and clear as one out of ten people seemed to be having fun while the countless others were deep in the midst of an existential crisis of dissatisfaction.

There came a day, I knew some of the simple lessons I'd learned needed to be captured in a book which led to a publishing deal. This then led me to much deeper work. My work was fueled by my own never-ending curiosity about what causes high-achievers to succeed, along with what was different for those specifically who maintained their quality of life.

When I began coaching high-achieving dentists, I quickly noticed similarities in many of their stories. Some people had come from war torn countries for example and who were told to go make something of themselves. Other dentists had parents who had pressed them hard, from a young age. Others were born into wealth with high expectations from their families. Although their circumstances varied, inevitably most had historically operated on overdrive. Almost all had suffered some form of childhood trauma, even if they hadn't realized it.

I've had doctors from all walks of life who told me their stories of struggle, pressure, and ultimately circumstances that seemed to cause the wiring of their brains to be "stuck" on overdrive. Most never wanted to stop growing and almost all were "nearly desperately" committed to their families' security. Meanwhile, I began to notice other recurring similarities of depression, feelings of inadequacy, burnout, frustration, and continual lack of understanding about why others in their circle of influence weren't always loyal and often appeared to lack integrity. Relationships were clearly strained.

Ultimately the high-achievers I coach or work with desire to live a fulfilled life with meaningful relationships. The question is how to balance their insatiable urge for growth with trust, ease and satisfaction.

What most dentists often don't realize is that there are simple options at their disposal that can help them operate in new ways with incredible efficiency. Ways that can make things effortless and even fun. Ways that can help them to lean into their greatest desires while growing personally and professionally leading to sustainable fulfillment and a legacy worth leaving.

Raving Referrals for Dentists provides some of the secrets to how high-achieving dentists can leverage their influence and begin to take back their quality of life.

What Will Your Story Be?

We want to help you massively transform your business and your life so that you have a compelling success story we can share with the world.

We hope you find so much value in our book and our *Referral Marketing System* that you too will share your story and our solution with others. After all, your story can inspire and motivate others to follow your steps and achieve the same results and success that you will have achieved.

We've combined all of the proven best practices in both marketing and referral generation into one fast, easy to use, and proven Referral Marketing System that will help you do three things:

1. Engage Your Referral Champions
2. Partner with Trusted Professionals
3. Promote Yourself and Your Team

Taking these three actions consistently will help you achieve top of mind awareness with your patients and social sphere that will generate referrals consistently. After all, your existing contacts and network already know hundreds, if not thousands, of people who fit your perfect prospect profile.

That's why we are going to teach you how to promote yourself and your services in a way that makes people view you as *THE* trusted solution they've been looking for to solve their dental challenges they face.

We'll teach you how to team up and partner with top professionals who already serve your ideal patients. Your strategic alliances will promote you to their best clients, colleagues, and social sphere as you follow our proven process.

Finally, our system will help you engage your relationships strategically to build instant rapport and deep trust. This will lead patients to trust you even more and ultimately refer you to their family, friends, co-workers, and colleagues, giving you all the business you could ever want.

We're Here to Help

We want to help you massively transform your practice and achieve the financial success and personal fulfillment you desire and deserve. As you read this book, you will find practical steps you can take to boost your business and attract more clients, but there are so many more factors to your success than just attracting new patients.

Our team at The Champions Institute has helped hundreds of dental practices grow their business which is exactly why we created our Champion Dentists program. This has quickly become the #1 pay-for-performance dental consulting and coaching program in the world, because our compensation is earned on actual performance, not promises.

We Want You to Retire Rich

Whether your goal is to increase new patient attraction, boost your case acceptance, or optimize your staff retention and loyalty, this program has been designed to maximize the valuation of your dental business.

That's important because in addition to the revenue you earn each month and each year, your goal should be to build a profitable practice you can sell for 10-15 times your EBITDA (Earnings Before Interest, Taxes, Depreciation and Amortization).

This productivity program uses a proprietary, process-driven, systematic approach to identify, evaluate and address key opportunities that drive your results. They use an advanced methodology that helps you generate lasting results increasing both your gross revenue and net profit quickly and consistently.

The Champion Dentists program helps you operate your dental practice at the highest level of performance and profitability. Those lucky enough to be chosen for this elite performance-based coaching and consulting program learn to elevate all aspects of operating your dental business.

Plus, Champion Dentist partners learn a proven leadership process to build a "Championship Culture" that elevates your staff productivity, happiness and loyalty. Best of all, this win-win program is delivered through a no-risk partnership agreement where you only pay after you experience results, and your revenue rises.

We invite you to schedule a complimentary profit optimization assessment call today to see how much additional revenue your practice is capable of.

Call us at **888-906-2070** or visit:
https://ChampionDentists.com

Chapter 1

What's Your Referral Score?

As you begin your journey towards achieving your Annual Income Goal, it's crucial to understand precisely where you are starting from and what gaps you might have in your current referral business practices.

If you study the top performers and producers in dentistry, you'll likely find that they all exhibit the same daily practices. By making a few minor changes to your daily habits, you can reach the same level of financial success that the top performers in dentistry have achieved.

As Dr. Len Tau says in his book Raving Patients,

> *"Word of mouth has always been the foundation for the acquisition of new patients by a dental practice."*

That's why we've developed a Referral Score assessment to help you understand how well you're currently performing in each of the ten daily practices that drive referrals.

This tool has been designed to identify quick and easy improvements to your business processes that can drive referrals for years to come.

Let's look specifically at the top ten actions that drive referrals and see how you measure up. As you review each practice, write down your self-assessed score on each of these daily practices. This will give you your baseline Referral Score and identify simple yet powerful opportunities for improvement.

Before you read on, scan this QR code
or use this link below for a special message about the
Raving Referrals Referral Score Quiz:

https://ravingreferrals.com/quiz/

#1 PLANNING YOUR SUCCESS

> *"Referrals can increase the income and influence of any dental practice. Having a solid strategy can make or break a business."*
>
> \- Holland Haiis
>
> Bestselling Author of Consciously Connecting

Every successful business owner has a detailed business plan for how they will achieve their goals and objectives. However, when it comes to referrals, this doesn't often hold true.

We're amazed how few professionals and even fewer dentists actually have a written plan that details exactly what they are going to do this week, this month, and this year to grow their referral business.

Considering the fact that over 65% of new business comes by referral, you are leaving money on the table if you don't have a written plan and system to drive referrals for your business.

Your plan should include your goals for the month, quarter, and year along with a detailed promotional plan and communication calendar, so you plan out your key offers and campaigns throughout the year.

How do you score when it comes to having a detailed business development and referral plan?

Rate yourself on a scale of 0-10, where 0 indicates you have no plan at all and 10 means you have a detailed action plan with written goals, promotions, and a communication calendar.

1. Planning ___________

#2 SERVING YOUR PATIENTS

When it comes to business, nothing matters more than serving your patients!

Providing exceptional service to each and every patient and community member should be the reason you do what you do. The money is simply the reward for a job well done!

The more exceptionally you serve your patients, the more referrals will flow your way. As people see how much you care about their success and satisfaction, they will naturally be more inclined to refer others to you.

On a scale of 0-10, how well do you score when it comes to serving your patients? Write down your score to practice #2 now.

2. Serving ____________

#3 ENGAGING PEOPLE CONSISTENTLY

The most successful professionals ensure they engage and connect with their most important relationships consistently.

As you invest time and energy in building strong relationships, you increase the number of people who know, like, and trust you enough to refer you to the people in their lives. The key is to engage them consistently while focusing on the things that matter most TO THEM.

After all, people don't care how much you know until they know how much you care. The more consistently you engage others personally and meaningfully, the more consistently they will recommend and refer you to their friends, family, colleagues, and social sphere.

So how do you score when it comes to connecting with and engaging people? Are you skillful at following up and building strong relationships, or do people rarely hear from you after they've met you for the first time?

Write down your score, with 0 being awful and 10 being masterful.

3. Engaging ____________

#4 ASKING FOR REFERRALS

We're often amazed how few dentists actually ask their patients or network for referrals. Most people in business understand that referrals drive their success, but often they feel awkward and uncomfortable asking for them. That's probably because they've never been taught when and how to ask for referrals in a way that makes your patients feel comfortable and happy to help.

We are going to teach you to master "The Art of the Ask" in Chapter 8. For now, be sure to write down your score of how consistent you are at asking for referrals from both your patients and professional colleagues.

4. Asking ____________

#5 TRACKING YOUR REFERRALS

The most successful dentists always measure and track their results, especially when it comes to referrals!

We're surprised how few people actually understand where their business comes from. After all, if you aren't tracking and measuring where each and every patient comes from, how can you expect to maximize your results?

Business experts teach, "What gets measured, gets maximized," and that is absolutely true. By tracking your referrals, you focus your mind on the #1 driver of your business success. The information you gather allows you to concentrate your valuable time and energy on your most productive and profitable relationships.

Okay, it's time to score how good you are at tracking the referrals you give and receive. Go ahead and write down your score now.

5. Tracking ____________

#6 THANKING PEOPLE WHO GIVE REFERRALS

Thanking people is a critical practice that can dramatically impact your success... if you do it consistently. Every time you receive a referral, you should be thanking the person who made the recommendation or introduction. Not only does this help them feel good because you've recognized them, but it also demonstrates your professionalism, which reinforces their feeling that recommending you was the right move to make.

Thanking referrers will dramatically boost their confidence in recommending you and improve the probability they send you more referrals in the future.

Please understand, this is one of the fastest and easiest ways to grow your referral business, so make sure you thank people each and every time they give you a new referral.

So how do you rate when it comes to consistently thanking people who give you referrals?

6. Thanking ___________

#7 UPDATING PEOPLE WHO GIVE REFERRALS

Updating people who give you referrals is another important practice that builds trust. People are highly appreciative when you call, text, DM, or email a quick update, letting them know if you were able to help their client, friend, or loved one.

This is especially true when the person giving you the referral is another professional. After all, they've entrusted their own personal credibility and relationship with their client to you. Following up with a quick update gives you a natural and comfortable opportunity to ask if they know anyone else who would benefit from your service.

If you've never even thought about updating people after they refer people to you, you may need to write down a score of 0 on this practice. On the other hand, maybe you are awesome at letting people know what's going on with the people they refer to you. If so, then write down a 10. Just be sure to write down your number so you can see your overall Referral Score.

7. Updating ___________

#8 REWARDING PEOPLE WHO GIVE REFERRALS

Rewarding your referral sources is another excellent business practice and catalyst for referrals, whether you incentivize people or simply surprise them with a gift when they refer you.

Some dentists design and promote a formal *Raving Rewards* program where patients and promotional partners are incentivized when they introduce prospects or potential new patients to your business.

We love *Raving Rewards* programs because they help create a culture of referrals. Plus, when designed properly, these programs automatically ask for referrals on your behalf without you ever having to leave your comfort zone.

Be sure to research and follow the regulations and restrictions for your industry, so you are always in complete compliance.

How good you are at rewarding people who give you referrals. Are you a 0, a 10, or somewhere in between?

8. Rewarding ____________

#9 RECOGNIZING PEOPLE WHO GIVE REFERRALS

Most people love to be publicly recognized for doing good work and helping others. In fact, our frail human ego has a very strong desire and need for recognition, especially in today's social media obsessed world of likes, shares, tweets, and follows.

That's why many dental practices grow rapidly once they start publicly celebrating and recognizing people who promote and refer them. Whether it be in the public areas of the business or through a newsletter, website or social media accounts, the social proof and credibility built by recognizing your referrers works quickly and effectively.

Be sure to get written permission from patients before acknowledging them publicly to comply with HIPAA regulations.

How about you? How well do you score when it comes to celebrating and recognizing the people who recommend and refer you? Write down your score so we can move to the final referral practice that drives your wealth.

9. Recognizing ___________

#10 PROMOTING YOURSELF AND YOUR SERVICES

Nearly 90% of business success comes down to your marketing and lead generation. After all, if you have enough sales and revenue coming in the door, most other problems can be solved. On the other hand, if you don't have a consistent flow of new and/or repeat patients, you don't really have much of a practice, do you?

After coaching, consulting, and working with thousands of businesses worldwide, we've found where most people fail is in their self-promotion and marketing efforts. Rather than attending events, networking, mailing out offers, or running ads online and off, many people simply do unprofitable "busy-work" that never gets them any closer to their Annual Income Goal. Whether that be because they are too busy, too shy, or just don't know-how, they simply don't invest enough time or money attracting new business opportunities.

How do you rate yourself in the marketing and promotion side of your practice?

If you are one of those people who always find a reason not to invest your time or money promoting yourself and your services, you may need to give yourself a 1, 2, or 3 on this practice. If you are a super promoter who always stays top-of-mind with your patients, fans, and followers, you should write down a 9 or a 10. Most people score between 3 and 5 on this one, so don't feel bad if you didn't score well on this important practice.

10. Promoting ____________

TIME FOR THE TALLY

Now for the fun part! Write down and add up each of your scores from the 10 referral best practices above.

1. Planning ________
2. Serving ________
3. Engaging ________
4. Asking ________
5. Tracking ________
6. Thanking ________
7. Updating ________
8. Rewarding ________
9. Recognizing ________
10. Promoting ________

TOTAL REFERRAL SCORE ____________________

Your Referral Score ranges from 0-100 and works just like a standard school grade. That means...

If you scored 90 or higher, you get an A

We'll bet you dollars to doughnuts that you are in the top 5% of income earners in your industry. You're probably already earning a great income and living the good life. You have solid systems in place that generate referrals consistently and automatically. Most likely, you take multiple vacations each year and share your abundance with everyone you love.

We hope every single one of our readers achieves this level of Referral Score after going through the training in this book and setting up your Referral Marketing System.

If you scored in this range, we congratulate and celebrate you. Well done!

If you scored between 80-89, you get a B

Most people who score this high are in the top 20% of income earners in dentistry. You likely have new referrals and opportunities coming to you on a daily basis and are doing quite well financially.

If you got a B on this test, you should feel proud for mastering so many of the referral best practices. Business must be pretty good, and your income is increasing. You're on your way, and it's just a matter of time before you blast through your Annual Income Goal.

If you scored between 70-79, your grade is a C

In the Olympics, third place still gets you on the podium, so feel proud of what you've accomplished thus far. Just know there's more work to do to reach gold medal status.

This is still a passing mark. You are likely in the top half of the producers in dentistry and are doing fine financially. You may have identified some opportunities for improvement as you reviewed these top 10 practices. Hopefully, you are now motivated to learn and apply the proven strategies, systems, and scripts we share in this book.

If you scored between 60-69, that means you got a D

If you're in this category, you're not alone. The majority of professionals initially get a failing *Referral Score* before they go through our program and apply our strategies. The knowledge and wisdom in this book can help you identify quick tweaks that help ramp up your revenue and maximize profitability.

If you are serious about growing your business and generating more income, just work on each of these daily practices and take consistent action. Fortunately, our easy-to-use system can help boost your score significantly.

If you scored below 60, you know what grade you got…

The optimists in us would tell you that scoring in this range just means you have many opportunities for improvement. Remember, this isn't your final grade. It's just the beginning. There is a lot you can do to quickly boost your *Referral Score* and your income.

The power behind building a business by referral is you actually compound your success once you start because more new patients refer more new patients who refer more new patients.

We're Here to Help

If you're feeling a bit stretched, stressed, or overwhelmed right now, we totally understand. Don't worry! We are committed to teaching you all you need to know to build a thriving practice.

You'll be retaking this test at the end of this book, so just focus on putting these methods to work in your practice, and you'll see your referrals and income start to rise.

If you haven't already taken your Referral Score Quiz online, scan this QR code or visit the link below to take the quick quiz now.

https://ravingreferrals.com/quiz/

Chapter 2

The 7 Laws of Raving Referrals

When it comes to generating Raving Referrals for your practice, there are seven laws you need to understand and master. When you build your practice in accordance with these seven laws, you will attract a steady stream of new patient opportunities for years to come.

Our goal is for you to get Raving Reviews just like this statement I recently heard about Dr. Steven Pohlhaus of Baltimore Center for Laser Dentistry. (LaserDentistBaltimore.com):

> *"I LOVE my dentist. So much so that I've stayed with him for 12 years and have referred to him countless times. I tell everyone about him. I've brought him a ton of new clients and recommended him to my friends, to all my coworkers, and even on Facebook to random people in our community who are looking for a new dentist."*
>
> \- *Nicole Poulous*

Raving Referral Law #1:

Every Referral Starts with Trust

The first thing you must understand when it comes to referrals is that every referral starts with trust.

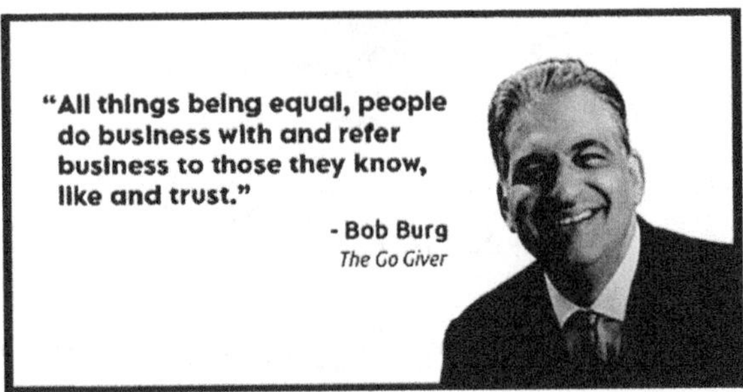

Think about the last referral, recommendation, or introduction you gave to a friend or colleague. How well did you know and trust the person you recommended?

Most likely, you trust them tremendously, or you would not have made that recommendation, right? If not, you gave the recommendation with a disclaimer saying something like, "I've never used them myself, but I hear they do a good job."

The same is true for everyone you know. The more they know, like, and ultimately trust you, the more they will sing your praises and passionately endorse you to the people in their lives.

In fact, your income is directly tied to the amount of trust that you build with your patients, colleagues, and social sphere. The more trust you earn, the more money you will earn over your career.

Gallup has conducted polls over the past several decades that consistently show that the most trusted professions on the planet are also the most highly paid, including doctors, engineers, and accountants.

The more people that trust that you are a person of integrity and an expert professional in your trade, the more confidence they will have in recommending you. Ultimately it is their trust in you that gives them the confidence to refer people they care about to you and your practice.

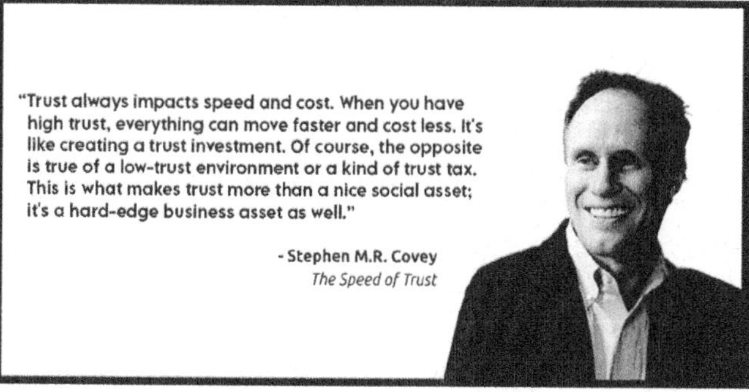

Raving Referral Law #2:

The More You Give, The More You Receive

Giving is the key that builds trust, deepens relationships, and unlocks referrals. Combining generosity into all that you do can show your patients how you are different than every other doctor out there. In fact, it can be one more powerful way to differentiate yourself from others in your field.

The more generous you are with your time, attention, understanding, and respect for others, the more liked and trusted you will become. In turn, people will go out of their way to help you succeed.

In life, there are people who take more than they give and those who give more than they take. Those who are constantly putting their own wants and needs first are typically viewed as selfish, egotistical, and greedy. Those who give generously tend to be viewed as noble, big-hearted, and even charitable.

So which camp do you want to be in?

Take a moment to think about the people in your life who are the greatest givers. Who are the three people you view as being most generous and giving of your family, friends, colleagues, and co-workers?

The 3 Most Generous People in My Life Are:

1. ____________________

2. ____________________

3. ____________________

How do you FEEL about the people you just identified? Does their generosity make you like them more?

Most likely, the answer is a resounding YES!

That's why when it comes to building trust, the more you give, the more you receive. Make it your mission to go out of your way to give your time, talents, attention, and best efforts in all you do.

Give your respect and attention to everyone you meet. Listen to them intently and ask probing questions about their passions and pursuits. Get to know what they really care about and help them achieve it if you can.

Give praise and public appreciation when people help you. Send them a thank you card, text, or testimonial for their business. When appropriate and while being mindful of privacy laws, give shoutouts on social media or via newsletters.

The more you give, the more referrals you will receive. So, give generously in all you do.

As Elijah "DJ Smiles" Desmond the founder of The Dental Festival and the Smiles at Sea dental cruise says,

> *"I over-deliver so much it makes people uncomfortable, so they have no choice but to give back by telling others about us."*

Raving Referral Law #3:

Relationships Trigger Transactions

You've probably heard the saying that people don't care how much you know until they know how much you care. As you build trust and give generously, you will strengthen and deepen relationships with people who have the ability to refer and recommend all the patients you will ever want or need.

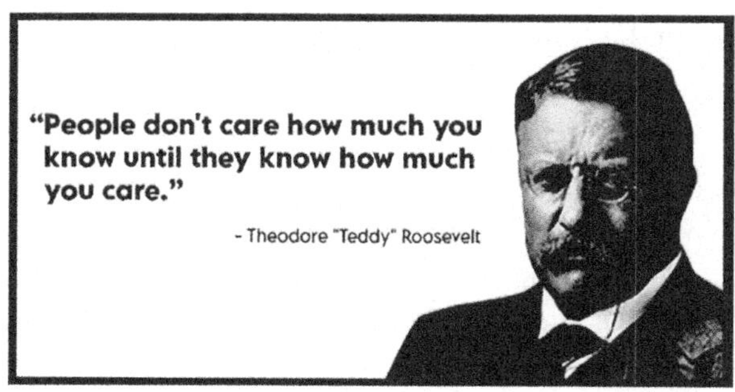

The reality is that trust only gets built through relationships. This is why the third law of Raving Referrals is that relationships trigger transactions. The quality of your relationships determines the quality of your life.

Before getting married, my wife and I went through a premarital course with the pastor of our church. One of the lessons he taught us was that relationships were like bank accounts. Every time you show someone you care about them, you make a deposit in that account, and your balance with them grows.

The more often you connect with the people in your life, the greater your relational equity with them will be. The better they get to know you, the more they start to like you and trust you, which then leads to them recommending and referring to you and your practice.

It makes sense, doesn't it?

Most banks charge service fees on inactive accounts, and the same thing happens with your relationships. The more time you let pass without communicating or connecting, your relational balance with that person declines.

If you don't reach out from time to time, they may actually forget about you altogether. They certainly won't be on the lookout for patients for you, which is what you want for your business.

That is why it's so important to continually engage and nurture all your Referral Champions, including your patients, referral partners, and social sphere.

Of course, it's always best to connect with people in person, because humans experience the strongest bonds when we are hanging out together having fun. That's why we recommend that you get together with your top relationships at least once every month or two.

That said, you can always send a text, call them on the phone, or send a personal message or handwritten note to show you are thinking about them. When you do, you are making relational deposits that will pay off big time once you learn the secrets to generating referrals.

The more personal your interactions are, the more relational equity you are creating. Remember that every touch counts. Even a quick text, email, direct message, social post, or newsletter will help you gain mindshare. Just remind your referral champions you are never too busy to help them and the people they care about. The more value you deliver to your relationships, the more frequently they will refer you.

Raving Referral Law #4:

Stellar Service Creates Stellar Success

The fourth law of generating Raving Referrals is that stellar service creates stellar success.

It should go without saying that the better you treat your patients, staff and assistants, the more success you will experience—both in terms of your personal income as well as your personal satisfaction and fulfillment.

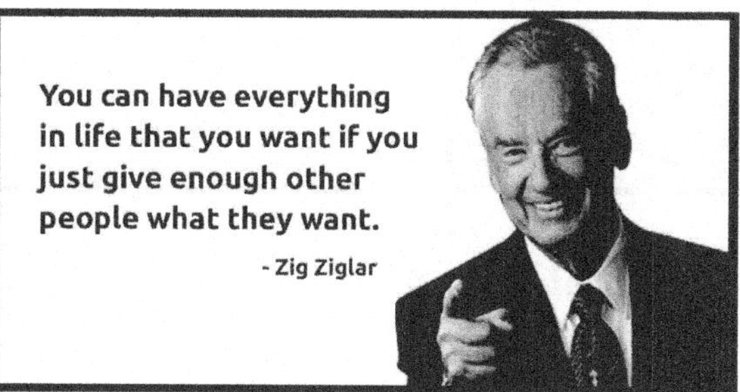

The more your patients and referral partners know how much you genuinely care about them and their success, the more they will care about you and your success.

The 5 Traits of Stellar Service:

When you serve patients exemplifying these five traits of stellar service, they will go out of their way to help you. In fact, they will rave about you each and every chance they get.

1. Listen intently to understand their cares and concerns
2. Communicate clearly
3. Meet and exceed expectations
4. Be on time and on budget
5. Always be in integrity

Be intentional about building a community of patients that are grateful for your service, generous with praise, and quick to recommend you to others. After all, word spreads quickly when you deliver stellar service to your patients. Soon, the only possible outcome is stellar success for you and your practice.

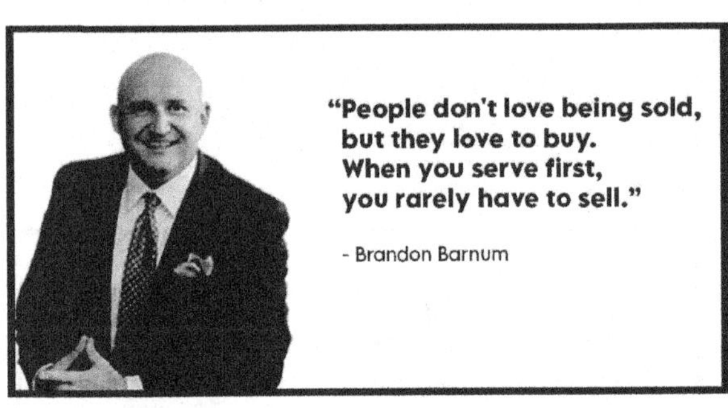

Raving Referral Law #5:

Delighted Patients Refer Delightful Patients

Wow your patients and referrals will follow.

The fifth law of Raving Referrals is that when you go above and beyond to delight your patients, they will happily and consistently refer you delightful patients.

Decades of empirical research shows that referred prospects:

- Trust you faster
- Refer more often
- Are more loyal
- Are more profitable
- Are more eager to choose you
- Are often pre-sold on switching to you
- Are more enjoyable to work with

When you add all of these factors together, it's no wonder why delighted patients refer delightful patients!

As your patients praise you to others, they actually transfer the trust they've built with others onto you. Every time that happens, your new patient's confidence in you and comfort with you grows.

Your goal should be for your patients to rave about you and your practice with so much reverence and appreciation that the people they promote you to have already decided to choose with you... even before you've ever heard their name.

Of course, converting Raving Referrals to delightful patients can only happen when you follow law number 6.

Raving Referral Law #6:

The Fortune is in the Follow-Up

When it comes to success for service businesses and professionals, your fortune will be made or lost based on how well you follow-up with people. In fact, follow-up is the single best way to double your referrals in a very short time.

Why? Because so few people actually do it. That means it's easy for you to stand out from your competition. Plus, it's a great demonstration of how well you follow-through and get the job done right.

If you really want a steady stream of Raving Referrals, you want to become famous for your follow-up.

Herbert True, a marketing specialist at Notre Dame University, found that:

- 44% of all salespeople quit following-up after the first call
- 24% quit following-up after the second call
- 14% quit following-up after the third call
- 12% quit following-up after the fourth call

That means 94% of all salespeople quit after the fourth call, yet 60% of all sales are made after the fourth call.

Plus, the more you update people as you serve them and the patients they refer, the more trust and confidence you build and the more referrals you will receive. Even if it's just a quick text, voice message, email, or social media message. Follow-up and watch the money start flowing to you faster.

If you really want to drive growth in your practice, follow-up with everyone who gives you a...

- Referral
- Introduction
- Testimonial
- Rating or Review

The more valuable the gift someone is giving you, the more important it is to follow-up with them. Be sure to thank them and give them updates so they have all the information they need and want.

As we mentioned earlier, when calculating your Referral Score, this practice is especially important when you receive a referral from a referral partner or professional colleague. When they trust you enough to serve their valuable clients, you have an incredible opportunity to deepen that relationship by following up with them. These updates demonstrate a high level of professionalism and continually build trust and collaboration.

Have your team call your partners with regular updates on the status of each patient they refer to you. That way, they will always know exactly how you are helping their clients.

It also gives you an opportunity to ask, "Is there anyone else you'd like us to help?"

According to Dr. Emily Letran DDS and CEO of Action to Win:

> *"Patient retention is one of the most important factors in growing a business because, over time, the patients who stay, pay, and refer are your greatest assets. Patient referrals should be leveraged as your number one marketing strategy."*

When you follow-up famously, you'll be amazed how many Raving Referrals you receive.

Raving Referral Law #7:

Everyone Wins, or No One Wins

The seventh and final law of generating Raving Referrals is that everyone wins, or no one wins.

When it comes to serving patients and building profitable partnerships with other professionals who serve your perfect prospects, it's important you ensure they always feel like they win every time they do business with you.

That requires that you strategically design your business practices, operations, and communications to guarantee that people know you have their best interests at heart.

Find ways to help them win.

Praise your patients, employees, and partners whenever possible. People love recognition, so give them a shout out in your newsletter, website, email, or social media accounts as appropriate.

Reward patients and referral partners who refer you so that they will feel honored, valued, and appreciated. This will boost the likelihood they will refer you again in the future.

Offer to cross-promote and recommend your partners to your patients, colleagues, and social sphere to help them attract more profitable prospects for their business.

The more people feel like they win every time they do business with you, the more business they will do with you... and the more Raving Referrals they will send your way.

To review, the 7 Laws of Raving Referrals are:

1. Every Referral Starts with Trust
2. The More You Give, The More You Receive
3. Relationships Trigger Transactions
4. Stellar Service Creates Stellar Success
5. Delighted Patients Refer Delightful Patients
6. The Fortune is in The Follow-Up
7. Everyone Wins, or No One Wins

As you master these seven laws and integrate them into your business, you will generate a steady stream of Raving Referrals for years to come.

For a quick summary of the 7 Laws of Raving Referrals, scan the QR code below or visit the link below:

https://ravingreferrals.com/7laws/

Chapter 3

Perfect Prospects & Lifetime Patients

Perfect Prospect Profile

Have you ever heard someone describe another person so vividly that you instantly thought of someone you know who's just like them? That's exactly what your goal is with your *Perfect Patient Profile.*

To empower others with the ability to refer quality patients quickly and consistently, you must create a *Service Statement* that paints a clear picture of precisely who you help and how you help them.

As you practice describing your *Perfect Patients* and your *Service Statement*, you can start sharing a clear, concise statement that will stick in the minds of people you meet. They will have no choice but to think of you the next time someone is describing the challenge that you solve.

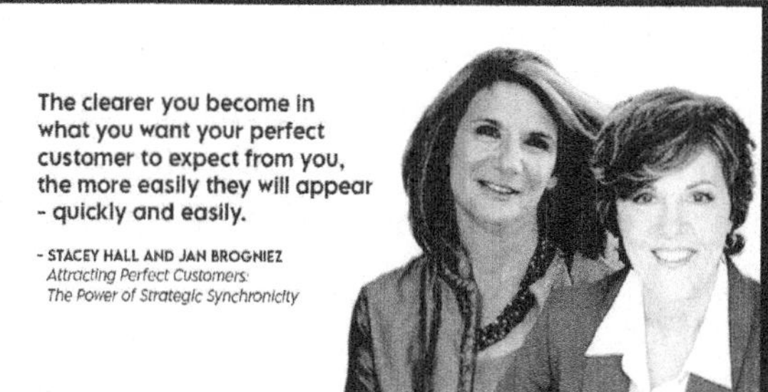

Quality Over Quantity

When it comes to referrals, it's better to have high-quality referrals to qualified candidates who actually need and want the service or solution you provide. You do not want to waste anyone's time so be clear on who your ideal patient is.

Your goal is to represent your *Perfect Patients* to referral partners, so they easily understand, remember, and scout for people who match your target. Your *Service Statement* gives them the ability to retell your story to others so their desire to do business with you increases before you've even spoken with them.

Once you've accomplished that, you will have enlisted them as Referral Champions scouting for you and singing your praises to the precise people you are looking to serve.

The Two Parts to Your Perfect Patient Profile Are:

1. Who you help
2. How you help

Once you get clear on these two things, the final step is to write your *Service Statement* and start sharing who you help and how you help as a story. That way people can tell your *Service Statement* and story each time they are talking to one of your Perfect Patients. So, let's go through each of these in detail, starting with who you help.

Who You Help

Take a moment to think about the best patients you've ever had throughout your entire career; the type of patient where if you could attract more exactly like these, you'd be beyond thrilled, and so would they.

Can you picture them right now? If I were to ask you the names of your five best patients, who would they be? Take a moment to write down their names now.

My 5 Best Patients Have Been:

1. ______________________________
2. ______________________________
3. ______________________________
4. ______________________________
5. ______________________________

What Makes Them Your Best Patients?

- Why did these people come to mind?
- What do they have in common?
- Were they your most profitable patients, the most enjoyable, or somewhere in between?
- Is there a specific type of patient who most benefits from your practice?
- What common goals, needs, or challenges do they share?
- What type of people give you the most referrals and introductions?
- How often do your ideal patients accept treatment?
- How much revenue do your ideal patients typically represent to you annually and over the lifetime of providing them care?

The answers to these questions should start to reveal some commonalities you can use to build your *Perfect Patient Profile*. The clearer that you are, the easier it is for others to refer to you effectively and consistently.

Maybe your ideal patient is a single mom in her 30s who loves yoga, cooking, and dancing. Or perhaps it is a grandparent over 60 who is getting ready to retire and relocate.

The more specific you are, the more clearly you can describe the type of people you are looking to serve. Your job is to make it easy for others to introduce and refer you to people who are a great fit for the services and solutions you provide. That will lead to more profitable prospects coming your way.

Diagnose Your Demographics

As you analyze your MVP patients, you will see that they share some of the same demographics. Take the time to review your most profitable patients from this or last year to assess and identify your *Perfect Patient Profile*: Evaluate them by the following demographics:

- Age
- Gender
- Income
- Location
- Stage of Life
- Marital Status
- Parental Status
- Homeownership Status
- Occupation, Hobbies, or Passions
- Typical Type of Insurance or Cash Paying

As you diagnose the demographics of your MVP patients, you will get clarity on your *Perfect Patient Profile* which you will use moving forward to refine your messaging and marketing.

How You Help

Once you have clarity around what your ideal patient looks like, next you need to define how you help them.

- What are the most common treatment problems you solve for your patients?

- What specific outcomes, goals, or objectives do you help your ideal patients achieve?
- What do you think is most important to your ideal patients?
- What are your best patient success stories?

According to Dr. Sean Mohtashami of 4M Institute and 4M Dental Implant Center,

> *"Understanding your perfect or ideal patient is to understand and realize patients' expectations. Make sure those expectations are realistic and achievable by the recommended treatment. Spending a little extra time with the patient, going through the challenges at hand, can save you headaches and misunderstandings down the line. Also, identifying patients' psychological issues is imperative to your long-term dental success. Realize that there are patients you will never be able to satisfy due to their psychological issues."*

It's important to both understand who you want to serve and how to best manage expectations. This will help you get clear on how best to describe the challenges you solve and the solutions you provide.

Write Your Service Statement

Once you've gotten crystal clear on who you help and how you help them, it's time to write your *Service Statement.*

This is a description of your practice you will share over and over in your community, on social media, at networking events, and professional functions. Your *Service Statement* will help paint a clear picture in the mind of the person you are talking to so they immediately think of people who might need your services.

We recommend you follow our DREAM formula to ensure your *Service Statement* is:

- Descriptive
- Relatable
- Engaging
- Authentic
- Memorable

Example Service Statement

To help you better understand what a powerful service statement looks like, here is an example of a Service Statement for a dentist:

> *"You know how some people are embarrassed smile and struggle with their confidence as a result of neglected care? Well, I help patients gain back their self-esteem with solutions that are painless and fans, giving them trans- formative results that can be life changing."*

In the example above, the dentist identified that she is looking to serve people lacking confidence as a result of poor dental care.

This gives the listener important data they can use to scan their memory banks and think about the people they know. Everyone has come across someone who has neglected their self-care with respect to their dental needs.

Once the listener meets someone who has this need in the future, they will quickly recall your scenario and recommend this person to you and your practice.

"The ability to sell is the number one skill in business. If you cannot sell, don't bother thinking about becoming a business owner."

- Robert Kiyosaki
Author of Rich Dad, Poor Dad

Get Started Now!

Take a few moments to describe a challenge that your ideal patients face. Then describe your solution in a way that tells a story the person will understand and remember. That way, they will immediately think of you and refer them to you.

Just fill in the blanks to create your *Service Statement*:

You know how ____
(Describe Your Ideal Patients and the Challenges the Face).

Well, I help ____

solve/achieve/give _____________________________________

Practice saying it out loud in the mirror once you've created a *Service Statement* you feel good about until it becomes completely comfortable and natural. Then, once you've mastered the mirror, ask a colleague or referral partner if you can share it with them. As you test it out on a few people, be sure to ask for their honest feedback.

Are there any refinements or improvements you want to make now that you've used it in a conversation and heard it out loud?

Was your statement clear as to who you help and how you help? Was it memorable? Ask them to restate what they heard so you can listen to how they describe your services.

Is there anyone they think of right now who matches your *Perfect Patients Profile*? You might just attract some Raving Referrals just by practicing your *Service Statement.*

As you practice and perfect sharing who you help and how you help with others, the more comfortably and powerfully you'll be able to share it. Over time, more and more people will understand exactly who you help and how you help.

Lifetime Patient Value

Each patient you serve is worth far more than the value of a single cleaning or consultation. After all, when you service your patients exceptionally well, they will depend on you for years to come and refer you to others frequently.

I learned that first-hand back in the mortgage business. Although I would earn an average of $3,000 per loan funded, I realized each client was really worth over $10,000 on average throughout the lifetime of each client relationship.

Clients would come to me for multiple loans over time, whether it be to buy a new home, refinance their existing home, or invest in a vacation or rental property. Plus, they would refer me to their friends, family, co-workers, and clients who I was happy to help.

To calculate out your *Lifetime Patient Value*, just multiple the average income you earn per visit, times the number of visits each patient averages with you, times the number of good referrals each patient gives you.

$ ________________Earnings Per Transaction

X _______________ # of Lifetime Transactions

X _______________ # of Referrals They Give

$ _______________ Lifetime Patient Value

For example, if your average transaction represents $250 per visit, and you service each patient once every 6-months (or 2 transactions per year), that patient is worth $500 to your business annually, assuming you're only providing routine hygiene.

If your typical patient uses your services an average of ten years, each patient then represents $5,000 in revenue over the lifetime of the patient engagement. That's not accounting for additional needs beyond hygiene such as whitening, crowns, veneers, clear aligners, dental implants and more. That's also not accounting for the fact that most patients end up bringing their entire family to a practice.

Referrals are the accelerator that really drives your revenue and business. If each patient refers you just one additional patient with a similar service plan, your initial patient has now delivered an additional $5,000 in projected revenue to your business not accounting for anything outside of hygiene.

Understanding the total value that each new patient represents to your business over time can change your perspective and appreciation for them in a hurry. It also determines how many marketing dollars you can afford to spend to acquire each new patient.

After all, if you could spend $250 to gain a patient worth $5,000 or even $10,000 to your business, how many times would you like to do that? As often as possible, right?

The key lesson here is to view each patient not just by the one-time revenue you will earn from servicing them today. Through the perspective of the lifetime patient value, you will earn by serving them and their referrals for years to come.

Danny Creed is a good friend of mine who also happens to be the six-time #1 global business coach for Bryan Tracy's Focal Point Coaching company. In Danny's book, *Thriving Business*, he states the five most common marketing mistakes are:

- No idea who the ideal customer (patient) is
- No idea what the ideal customer (patient) wants
- No idea as to what business you're really in
- No idea why anyone should buy or what sets you apart from the competition
- No idea how to explain your business in thirty seconds or less

If any of those is a gap for you, take a few minutes to get clear on each of these five areas of your business.

Before long, you'll have Raving Referrals and introductions coming in consistently.

Creating your *Perfect Patient Profile* is an important step towards success. Scan the QR code or visit the link below to view a special video tip:

https://ravingreferrals.com/perfect_prospect

Chapter 4

Learn Why They Buy

For many dentists, case acceptance can be a challenge. So, what if there was a quick, easy, and effective way to increase your closing rate up to 300%?

There is when you learn people's **BANK**CODE and understand how each person thinks and how they make buying decisions.

The truth is that we human beings have twenty-four very different personality styles. Some people are naturally outgoing and friendly, greeting everyone they meet with a smile and a hug. These people excel in sales, customer service, and other positions where relationships matter.

Others are shyer and more introverted, preferring to have as little human contact as possible. You probably know a number of these people, and perhaps that is how you were created. These people tend to be computer programmers, accountants, mechanics, electricians, plumbers, and other professions where they can excel working with things more than with people.

Take It to The B.A.N.K.

When it comes to the buying process, the same is true. When working with patients and offering or presenting treatment, some will use their intuition to assess your offer quickly. Others need time to analyze information on their various options to select the optimal solution before moving forward.

It's important to recognize people think differently based on their personality style. So, if people process information and make decisions much differently, why do most businesspeople use the exact same presentations and conversations for each prospect they meet?

This was a question I had never considered until October 14, 2017, when I was leading a 2-day event called the **Profit Partner Summit** teaching this Raving Referrals system to an audience of over 200 in Phoenix, Arizona. After walking off stage, a woman named Sandy approached me, introduced herself, handed me four colored cards, and said,

> *"Do me a favor: read the information on these cards and sort them in the order of what's most important to least important to you. That will help me serve you better and save us both time."*

After reviewing the cards, I quickly sorted and handed them back. What happened next blew me away.

As Sandy reviewed the order of the cards I handed her, she started describing my personality. I was shocked at how accurate her assessment was, and all I had done was sort four cards. I've taken at least a dozen different personality assessments, including Myers Briggs (MBTI), DiSC, The Harrison Assessment, and StrengthsFinder, to name a few. Each time, I had to go online and tediously answer 60-100 questions which typically took between 10-20 minutes. With **B.A.N.K.,** it was nearly instant, and there was no technology needed.

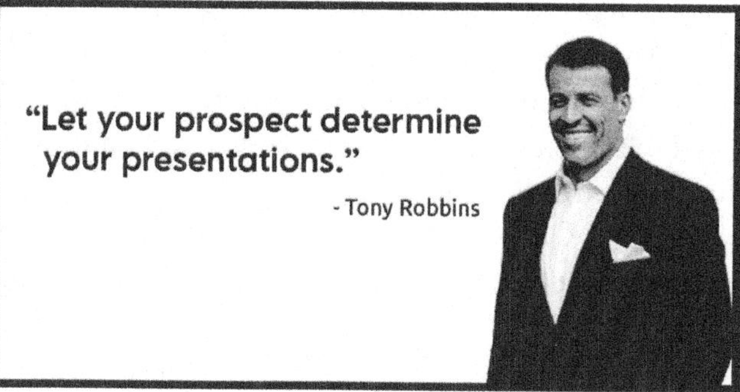

Sandy went on to explain how this **B.A.N.K.** system helps you close more sales in less time, increasing closing rates to as much as 300%. She also shared a white paper scientifically validating **B.A.N.K.** as the world's only sales methodology that accurately predicts buying behavior in real-time.

Close More Sales in Less Time

The key to increasing your sales conversion rates is to identify your prospect's personality type. Once you understand their **BANK**CODE you can customize your conversations and presentations to be most effective based on how each person processes information and makes buying decisions. In just seconds, this easy and reliable system can help you:

- Supercharge Your Treatment Presentation
- Transform Your Communications
- Make Lifelong Connections
- Empower your team to support you

Science long ago determined that four distinct primary personality types explain how we think, make decisions, and interact with the world. **B.A.N.K.** uses this personality science to help you improve interpersonal communication for better personal and professional relationships.

In 1992, the Chally Group conducted a research project known as the World Class Sales Project. They concluded that only 18% of buyers would buy from a salesperson who doesn't match the buyer's personality type. That's much lower than the 82% success rate when personality types are aligned.

The four **BANK**CODES are: Blueprint, Action, Nurturing, and Knowledge.

As you look at the following list, which would you choose as your top choice if you could only choose one?

BLUEPRINT	ACTION	NURTURING	KNOWLEDGE
Stability Structure Systems Planning Processes Predictability Responsibility Duty Rules Credentials Titles Tradition	Freedom Flexibility Spontaneity Action Opportunity Excitement Attention Stimulation Competition Winning Fun Image	Relationships Authenticity Personal Growth Significance Teamwork Involvement Community Charity Ethics Harmony Morality Contribution	Learning Intelligence Logic Self-Mastery Technology Research & Development Science Universal Truths Expertise Competence Accuracy The Big Picture

Now that you've identified your first choice, what would you choose next? Complete that process until you have your four- code combination and write that in the lines below:

____

____

____

____

Unlike other personality systems that are based on psychology, **B.A.N.K.** is the only values-based assessment that measures a person's "buyology." My fascination grew after Sandy emailed my 24-page **BANK**PASS report, which explained my personality in great detail. It outlined the triggers which get me to yes and the tripwires that lead me to say no in a sales setting. Beyond that, it helped me understand how to better connect and communicate with the other codes I had struggled with before.

Did you know there are 24 individual **BANK**CODES that drive why people buy? To learn the secrets, science and system to increase sales conversions up to 300%, visit:

https://ravingreferrals.com/bankcode/
or Scan the Code Below:

Instant Empathy

The market researcher in me needed to test the system and see what results it delivered. As I started using the cards at networking events and one-on-one meetings, I found people were as fascinated as I was. Each person I handed the cards to was happy to participate because the exercise was all about them. They were excited to share why they chose each card. It was amazing to watch these colorful cards quickly identify each person's personality in under 90 seconds.

What I soon realized was that **B.A.N.K.** gave me instant empathy. Within seconds of meeting someone, I cracked their code and immediately understood how their mind works. Best of all, it's fast, fun, and fascinating. People love talking about themselves, which creates the space where people open up, helping you understand them rapidly.

> *"Growing your business is all about relationships. You never start out talking about dentistry. People want to do business with people they like. When you build your practice around positive relationships you've built, your practice becomes a refuge."*
>
> *- Dr. Dennis Smiler*

The most important code I ever cracked was for my daughter Ella. While we are incredibly close and have great daddy-daughter dates, our conversations have felt more like debates since she entered her teen years.

After cracking her **BANK**CODE and watching her select the Knowledge card first, everything suddenly clicked. Our codes are complete opposites, which helped me understand the space between us. Instantly I saw how my way of expressing myself completely repelled her because it didn't match the way her brain processes information. When we talk, her scientific mind goes to work analyzing for accuracy and application. If I make grandiose or generalized statements, her natural response is to question or challenge, which leaves me feeling criticized.

Because of **B.A.N.K.,** I now understand my daughter much better. Rather than trying to change her, I embrace and celebrate her strengths. Seeing her choose the Nurturing card last helped me understand why she rarely shows affection like she did when she was young. Now that I understand how her brilliant brain works, I truly appreciate the woman she was created to be.

It's been years since cracking Ella's code, and our relationship has never been better. I'll be forever grateful for the understanding and empathy **B.A.N.K.** has given me.

Referred to a Rockstar

Since this book is about generating Raving Referrals, I have to share that I was thrilled when Sandy called offering to introduce me to Cheri Tree, the creator of the program and author of the book, ***Why They Buy***.

Over a series of phone calls, Cheri and I became fast friends and mutual admirers. Before long, we were collaborating and creating a strategic alliance to empower more people with **B.A.N.K.** We scheduled an interview and promoted her to my tribe. Then, as our respect and relationship grew, Cheri invited me to teach the Raving Referrals system to her audience at the international **B.A.N.K.** conference in Vegas. The following month, I invited her to join me at an Oscars after party at Universal Studios in L.A. with Ashton Kutcher and Matthew McConaughey as guests of honor.

Over the years that have followed, my respect and admiration for Cheri have grown immensely, and I believe the feeling is mutual. In my opinion, **B.A.N.K.** can help everyone improve their relationships and live better lives. That's why I am committed to supporting Cheri's mission to crack the code of every person on the planet.

To that end, I dedicated ten months of my life to helping her build and launch Codebreaker Technologies, including Codebreaker AI. This revolutionary technology enables you to crack personality codes in just one click using a LinkedIn profile. It's an amazing tool that I recommend to anyone looking to close more sales and build better relationships.

One of the reasons I share this example is that being referred to as influencers is a strategy you want to master. This will help you gain access to people you may otherwise never meet. In today's hyper-social world, just one referral can change your life.

The key is to follow up and follow through. Add value and help achieve whatever mission, dream, or goal they are passionate about. Then when you earn an influencer's trust and have given them tremendous value, they will feel indebted and naturally offer to promote. When they do, their celebrity endorsement elevates your expert status, which in turn boosts your referrals and revenues.

To unlock the secrets, the science, and the system to supercharge your sales in less than 90 seconds,

Visit **KnowYourCode.US** or scan the QR code below:

Chapter 5

Elevate Your Expert Status

Elevating your expertise in a specific or niche area of dentistry is one of the most strategic ways to build your practice. It increases your credibility and visibility, which helps attract new patients and referral partners. Plus, if you don't share your expertise online, your competitors will be happy to step in and win over your patients.

When you look up the word "expert" in the Oxford dictionary, you'll find the definition reads, "a person who has a comprehensive and authoritative knowledge of or skill in a particular area."

While you may not want to claim you are an expert in only one area of dentistry, the truth is you have specialized knowledge with select treatments that you likely love providing more than others. The saying is, "when you niche you get rich". So, consider what services in particular you could focus on as an expert in your marketing.

One of the many inspiring authors I've had the pleasure of knowing is Debbie Allen, author of the book, *The Highly Paid Expert.* Debbie truly is an expert on becoming an expert. In her 2019 book, *Success Is Easy*, Debbie shares,

> *"What's great about being an expert is that while you are fulfilling your life's mission, you are also influencing and teaching others. As the expert, you can go deeper with your knowledge than the average*

> *person in your industry and develop a step-by-step blueprint, program, or system that can be duplicated by other people."*

To establish your expertise, consider posting and promoting the following on your website and social media channels, as well as displaying them throughout your office:

- Affiliations with Chambers of Commerce or the Better Business Bureau
- Articles or blogs you have written
- Associations to which you belong
- Awards you have received
- Boards on which you serve
- Books you have written or have been featured in
- Charities for which you volunteer or committees on which you serve
- Endorsements from vendors or suppliers
- Media interviews or coverage you have received
- Partners who have chosen to do business with you
- Photos with celebrities, authors, and influencers
- Testimonials from patients

In addition to posting and displaying these examples of your expertise, you can also go live on social media, sharing quick tips for your *Perfect Patients*. While it may seem intimidating at first, here's a simple formula you can follow to share your expertise:

- Introduce yourself, stating your name and practice name
- Describe the most common or primary challenges you solve
- Emphasize the pain of not taking action
- Outline top options and solutions
- Share success stories
- Suggest next steps

Here's an example script to give you some ideas,

"Hello, this is Dr. Andrews with Andrews DDS, here to give you my top five tips for people feeling self-conscious due to bad breath. I love helping patients discover how different they become when they feel comfortable with their own oral hygiene and smile.

The challenge many people face is that they don't know there are lasting solutions which can give them back their confidence. Here are three tips to help you take back your confidence.

- *Always smile no matter what!*
- *Understand that there are multiple options to help change your oral health in a short amount of time.*
- *Many options to change your bad breath can be accomplished for little cost and pain free.*
- *Bad breath is completely curable.*
- *A free consultation is offered at our practice where our team is mindful of your challenge and is used to many people who are in your shoes.*

These tips are great reminders even if you have already seen a dentist who told you this was going to be an ongoing or incurable issue.

We are here to help and am never too busy to take care of people who care about their oral health. Just have them call or text me at (123) 456-7890.

Thanks for watching, and remember, at Andrews DDS, we're committed to helping you reach your oral health care goals."

If you're not sure where to start, simply search online for articles related to dentistry. You will find countless books, blogs, strategies, and tips you already know and can easily teach your patients or network.

Now it's time to share that wisdom with the world. As you post your golden nuggets, you'll find that your patients and the social sphere will engage, ask questions, and request more information about your services. As if by magic, new patient opportunities will appear as if they are drawn to you like a magnet. People you've never met will also share what you do with others, especially as you tell stories of the impact you make.

You can elevate your expert status by creating a blog, podcast, video, special report, workshop, webinar, or book. The key is to constantly share your knowledge and wisdom so you stay top of mind and elevate your status with everyone you can.

One of the most significant benefits of sharing your expertise on social media is that other influencers and business owners will ask to interview you to help their clients and social sphere. As they do, you may find some of them make excellent guests sharing their expertise with your audience. This is one of the most powerful strategies you can use to grow your referrals, which is why we will cover it in detail in Chapter 16 of this book as we outline the top *21 Top Cross Promotion Campaigns.*

If you are at a place where you feel like you could use a coach to help you come up with the clarity and a strategy needed to take your influence to the next level, consider hiring an influence coach. An

Influence coach is someone who helps you to create a straightforward plan that can be easily implemented to take your expert status to the next level. This combined with ongoing check-ins can help guide you in executing the highest priorities needed to meet your benchmarks. Anyone who has excellence in their particular field undoubtedly has a coach. This is no different in dentistry. For more on how to leverage your influence with a coach, visit https://influentialdentists.com/.

Be Easy to Refer

To maximize the quality and quantity of Raving Referrals coming your way, it's critical you make yourself easy to refer.

Giving your patients, referral partners, and social sphere an easy way to recommend, refer, and promote you is one of the fastest ways to grow your business.

When you think about your practice, why would someone tell another person about you?

The answer is likely different than you imagine. The fact of the matter is most people don't care about you or your practice the way you do. Their motivation for recommending you is primarily to solve the problems and challenges for the people they care about. Your job is to make it quick and easy for them to spread the word about your practice far and wide so you can attract as many potential patients as possible.

When people have a referral for you, what are you asking them to do?

If you're sitting there stymied by that question, that means you have a big gap in your business. You are making them do all the work and creating barriers between you and your ideal patients. The simple truth is that business development is your job. So why would you make others work to give you business?

Consider creating a referral card that gives your referral partners your website, phone number, social media, and a QR code they can scan with their mobile phone. Here's an example you can follow:

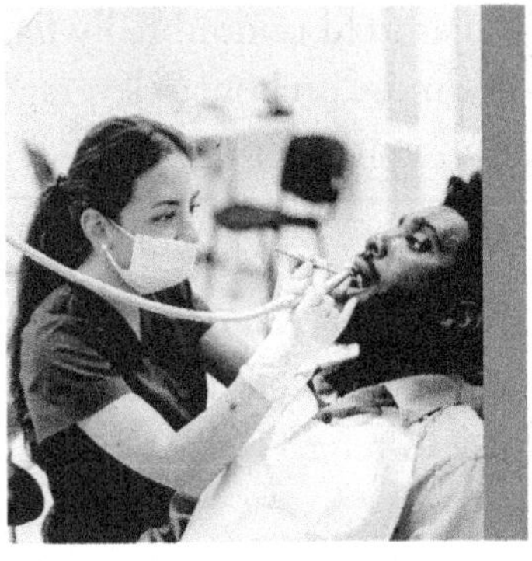

One of the biggest gaps I see when coaching clients to get more referrals is that they have no system in place for their referrals. I've surveyed thousands of business owners and found that less than 10% actually have a system in place to ask, receive, track, and follow up on the referrals they receive.

That means nine out of ten of you have a serious gap that is costing you money each and every day. That's why you need to develop a Referral Kit for your business.

Your Referral Kit

Your *Referral Kit* is something tangible you give your patients and referral partners to share when recommending you. Simply package your expertise as a special report, book, video, or brochure that explains the challenge you solve, the possible solutions clients should consider, and a specific call-to-action, so they contact you for assistance. This elevates your authority in the mind of your patient, which instantly boosts trust.

Your Referral Kit will increase the number of prospects you attract while simultaneously boosting your average revenue per patient once they view you as a trusted expert for a particular treatment or niche.

The good news about creating your Referral Kit is that you only have to do it once, and you can use it for the rest of your career. The easiest way to create your Referral Kit is to compile blogs you've written into a book or special report. If you haven't written any blogs, you can use the Frequently Asked Questions section of your website to get started.

Another great option is to record an interview and have the audio recording transcribed. Simply coordinate a conversation with one of your business or referral partners via zoom or Facebook Live.

Then download the video file and upload it to one of the many online transcription services like Temi.com or Otter.ai.

Once you package and publish your expertise through your Referral Kit, you boost your influencer status, which will lead people to seek you out. After all, your Referral Kit elevates your status from being seen as an average dentist to an industry expert.

That was my experience after Mark Victor Hansen and Robert Allen featured me in their best-selling book, *Cracking the Millionaire Code*, back in 2005. Once that book was published, I had prospective clients calling and contacting me from around the world. They were eager to do business with me because these global authorities and influencers had established my expertise before I had ever spoken with these people. Sixteen years later, people still reach out to me after reading that book.

Give the Gift of You

The goal of your Referral Kit is to give your referral champions a turn-key tool they can use to promote your services easily, effortlessly, and effectively. When they share your Referral Kit, you educate your audience, elevate your status, and reduce sales pressure. These factors all attract profitable prospects who will schedule with you quickly and consistently.

You can even present your Referral Kit as a gift. Once you package your expertise in a special report or book, your referral partners can give it as a gift for each of their clients and customers. They are looking to help and add value to their clients, so if you give them a way to do that by introducing your expertise, it creates a win–win–win scenario where everyone benefits.

That's exactly what I did with *Cracking the Millionaire Code*. That book became my personal brochure. Every time I met a new prospect, I gave them a copy of the book along with my business card inserted on page 42, where my three-page bio began. Even if they never read a word of the book, the simple fact that these literary giants had endorsed and written about me established my expertise and trustworthiness. Plus, it became an easy way for people to recommend me to their clients and contacts.

Creating your own Referral Kit and elevating your expertise will elevate your status and accelerate trust. The key is to make it easy for others to refer to you in a way that makes you the most trusted option in the eyes of your partners and prospects. Once you do that, you are on your way to attracting Raving Referrals for years to come.

That truly is the beauty of this Raving Referrals program. As you put this system and these strategies to work in your practice, you will build a growing group of referral partners and loyal patients who will gladly refer ideal prospects to you quickly and consistently.

The Appreciation Challenge

Giving is the key that unlocks receiving. The more you give, the more you will receive.

Be on the lookout for ways to give to people you care about and those you're looking to build profitable partnerships with or attract referrals from. The more time and energy you invest in your key connections and meaningful relationships, the more relational equity you build, which will generate opportunities for years to come.

One of the fastest, easiest, and most powerful things you can do to add value is to simply appreciate them. That's why we challenge you to show some appreciation right now.

The Rules:

- Look through the contacts on your mobile phone.
- Choose the top 10 people you want to build relational equity with.
- Text or send a direct message or personalized video expressing your genuine appreciation for them.
- Complete this exercise within 1 hour of reading these instructions.
- Don't ask anything of them in return. Just give them some gratitude and appreciation.
- Don't even ask them to respond to you. It's as easy as that!

Appreciation Examples:

- Been thinking about you and wanted you to know how
- much I appreciate you.
- Thanks for all you are and all you do. I appreciate you!
- Someone asked me to think of people I appreciate, and you immediately came to mind. Just wanted to let you know I appreciate you. Have a great day.
- Thank you for always ________________. I appreciate you.
- Have I told you lately you inspire me?
- I just wanted you to know I was reading some of your social posts and really appreciate how you show up in the world.

- I thought you would like to know I was just thinking about the people I admire most, and you are at the top of my list. Thanks for being you.
- I just wanted you to know how much I respect and admire you. You inspire me.

As you text your expressions of appreciation, you'll be amazed at the response you will receive. People will be blown away because they don't hear unsolicited praise very often. As you show your appreciation for them, they will naturally thank you for your kind words. Often, this will lead to opportunities to connect and discuss the possibility of a profitable partnership.

So have fun and spread the love right now!

Seriously. Stop reading and **DO THIS RIGHT NOW.** It's one of the easiest ways to quickly start a conversation with someone you admire who can make a difference to you personally and professionally. It only takes a few minutes, so put a bookmark on this page and spread the love. You'll be glad you did, and so will those you reach out to.

Now that we've covered the Raving Referral basics, it's time to give you the secrets and the science to engaging and activating your referral network, so they become your referral champions.

Scan the QR code or visit the link below for quick tips on establishing your expert status:

https://ravingreferrals.com/expertise

Chapter 6

Engage Your Referral Champions

As a practice owner, the level of your success is mainly dependent on your ability to attract Raving Referrals. The more recommendations you receive from patients and your social sphere, the faster your business will grow and the more prosperity you will achieve. That's why it's so important to engage your network systematically in a way that transforms them into Referral Champions for you and your business. Then, the more you celebrate, thank, and reward your Referral Champions, the more Raving Referrals you will receive.

Most practice owners struggle their entire career trying to attract patients by marketing to strangers. They spend tens of thousands of dollars on ineffective marketing, wasting hundreds of hours talking to people who will never deliver any real value to their business.

The truth is that you're sitting on an untapped goldmine of ideal patients you can access quickly and serve consistently. This section will share a time-tested way to have your network deliver patients to you on a silver platter.

Even if you struggle with networking and are uncomfortable promoting yourself, the system, strategies, and scripts outlined here will give you a simple and scalable way to create predictable profitability for your practice.

**Who do you know,
Who knows people,
You want and need to know?**

The 3 Sources of Raving Referrals

The vast majority of referrals come from one of the following three groups of people:

1. Your Patients and team
2. Your Social Sphere
3. Complimentary Businesses and Professionals

Each of these groups can be an incredible source of referrals. While each group needs a slightly different approach to activate them into Referral Champions for your business, the overall strategy is very similar.

Your Patients

Current and past patients can be your #1 best source of referrals. That's because they have personally experienced and benefited from your services. When they share their story, and testimonial about the difference you made for them, the people they recommend to you automatically trust you more, which increases the likelihood they will use your service.

The key here is to consistently communicate to your patients through phone calls, text messages, email, direct mail, social media messages, and patient appreciation events, so they feel the love over and over. Then, when you hear someone is looking for the service you provide, they will naturally and passionately recommend you and your practice.

Your Social Sphere

> *"Referrals are critical for your business. I built my New York practice by connecting with my community. Some of my best referrals came from having lunch at the local diner or deli and building friendships with the local community. As a member of Rotary, BNI, the chamber of commerce and my local temple helped me win influential patients including the mayor, fire chief and police chief of my town which led to an endless stream of referrals. Plus, hosting charity events elevated my visibility and created trust and loyalty amongst my patients and social sphere."*
>
> Edward Feinberg DMD
> Lake Pleasant Dentistry
> TheOnwardProgram.com

Your social sphere includes all the people you interact with in your life, including your friends, family members, co-workers, and contacts. The truth is you should be promoting your services to everyone who is in your contact relationship management (CRM), email programs, phone contacts, and social media connections.

Imagine how many more referrals you would attract to your business if you just stayed in touch with all the people you have met and hired for various services in your life. You are literally three feet from gold, and it's time you started mining it.

As you look over the list on the following two pages, start thinking about people you know in each of these industries and categories:

- Accountants
- Account Managers
- Advertising Managers
- Appliance Repair People
- Appraisers
- Architects
- Athletes
- Attorneys
- Authors
- Auto Mechanics
- Babysitters
- Bakers
- Bankruptcy Attorneys
- Bartenders
- Bookkeepers
- Business Brokers
- Business Coaches
- Business Development Managers
- Business Managers
- Business Owners
- Career Coaches
- Carpet Cleaners
- Car Salespeople
- CEOs
- Charities
- Chefs
- Chiropractors
- Church Members
- College Alumni
- Concierges
- Consultants
- Contractors
- Copywriters
- Counselors
- Credit Repair Experts
- Cyber Security Experts
- Daycare Providers
- Dentists
- Divorce Attorneys
- Dog Groomers
- Drycleaners
- Drywallers
- Endodontists
- Engineers
- Entrepreneurs
- Escrow Officers
- Estate Planning Attorneys
- Event Managers
- Executives
- Family Members
- Financial Planners
- Firefighters
- First Responders
- Flooring Installers
- Florists
- Franchise Consultants
- Friends
- Fundraisers
- Furniture Salespeople
- Golf Pros
- Goverment Employees
- Graphic Designers
- Grocers
- Hair Stylists
- Handymen
- Health Coaches
- Healthcare Professionals
- High School Friends
- Home Builders
- Home Healthcare Providers
- Home Inspectors
- Hotel Managers

House Cleaners
Human Resource Managers
Influencers
Insurance Agents
Interior Designers
Investors
Jewelers
Landscapers
Leasing Agents
Life Coaches
Manicurists
Marketing Consultants
Mediators
Mortgage Loan Officers
Movers
Musicians
Nurses
Nutritionists
Office Managers
Optometrists
Oral & Maxillofacial Surgeons
Orthodontists
Painters
Paramedics
Pastors
Pediatric Dentists
Pediatricians
Periodontists
Personal Trainers
Pest Control Technicians
Pharmacists
Photographers
Plumbers
Police Officers
Politicians
Pool Cleaners
PR Agents
Printers
Programmers
Project Managers
Property Managers
Prosthodontists
Public Speakers
Real Estate Agents
Relationship Managers
Rental Agents
Reporters
Restaurant Owners
Roofers
Salespeople
Sales Trainers
Secretaries
Security Guards
Seminar Attendees
Skin Care Specialists
Social Media Consultants
Software Designers
Surgeons
Swimming Instructors
Tax Advisors
Teachers
Technology Experts
Tennis Pros
Travel Agents
Veterans
Veterinarians
Virtual Assistants
Waiters and Watresses
Web Designers
Writers
Yoga Instructors
Youth Sports Coaches

As you look over this list, you're undoubtedly thinking of people you know who should know about your business. If you have their contact information, start communicating with them regularly about the products and services you provide. After all, you never know when they or someone they know will need what you offer. If you aren't marketing to them consistently and staying top-of-mind, someone else will be glad to serve them and win their business.

You may be looking at this list thinking, "I would never want to approach these people about my business." If so, that may be part of the reason you don't yet have the results you desire and deserve. Don't let your ego get in the way of your success. This is not the time to be shy. Your family's future success is at stake. Be confident and bold, knowing you provide great value to everyone you serve.

I learned long ago that you could either be right, or you can be rich. It's your choice, so choose wisely. If you are committed to success, spread the word far and wide about the services you provide. After all, nothing ventured, nothing gained.

You have absolutely nothing to lose. If you email or contact people and they aren't interested in doing business with you, they will simply ignore your message and move on. That said, by keeping your name and brand top of mind, they are much more likely to use your services and recommend you in the future.

Complementary Businesses and Professionals

While your past patients and social sphere are incredibly important, in my experience, you can build your business exponentially faster and larger by partnering with complementary business owners and professionals who serve your ideal patients. This strategy is so powerful that over half of this book is dedicated to teaching you how to achieve wealth and prosperity by partnering and cross- promoting with people who are serving your perfect patients each and every day.

As you look back at the Social Sphere list we just covered, you probably see at least ten industries or professions that make their living serving the exact patients you are looking to attract. All you need is one solid partnership in each of those industries to create predictable profitability for your business.

I've personally closed over $500 million in business using this strategy, so I am here to tell you emphatically that it works when you work it. As a single dad back in my twenties, I was earning over $50,000 per year from just one referral partner alone. Imagine what you can achieve for your business when you follow the Raving Referrals system and *Referral Partner Blueprint* to create ten or more referral partnerships over the next year or two.

By collaborating and co-marketing with these people, you will help them grow their business while they help you grow yours.

Best of all, as you prove yourself to them and their clients, you will become an invaluable ally they can't live without. You will earn more and more of their business over time until, eventually, you will become the number one go-to expert to which they refer all of their clients and colleagues.

Your Network Drives Your Net Worth

We will teach you more about creating profitable partnerships including potential cross-promotional campaigns you can deploy with your referral partners in later chapters. First, let's cover how to build your database and stay top of mind with each of the three sources or Raving Referrals.

Compile Your Database

If you're serious about success, building a database of your past patients, complementary professionals, and social sphere is paramount. All of your contacts should be centralized in one contact relationship management (CRM) system to make it easy for you to consistently communicate with your network. This could even be your practice management software.

Create Lifetime Patients

If you are serious about winning patients for life, it's imperative you keep your brand top-of-mind. Your goal is to become the top trusted solution in your industry, so people always use your services and tell everyone they know to do the same.

Once your contacts are centralized, be sure to schedule a regular message to your market every month at a minimum. Consistently keep your brand and services in front of your database through regular printed or emailed newsletters as well as through your social media channels.

Here are some great segments and ideas for what to feature in your newsletters and social posts:

- Articles and Blogs
- Awards and Recognition
- Charity Collaborations
- Patient Appreciation Events
- Patient Success Stories
- Community Impact Campaigns
- Practice Announcements
- Holiday Highlights
- Industry Updates
- Inspirational Quotes
- In-House Plan Opportunities
- New Employee Introductions
- Product and Service Announcements and Training
- Referral Partner Spotlights
- Raving Rewards
- Referral Shout-Outs

- Special Offers
- Technology Innovations
- Testimonials
- Tips and Tricks
- Training Events
- Trends and Statistics

We will go into detail on how to communicate and cross-promote to your network in a later chapter. For now, the key is to schedule a regular message or newsletter to your database at least once per month. With any public shout-outs, always get permission in writing if the person you're acknowledging is a patient.

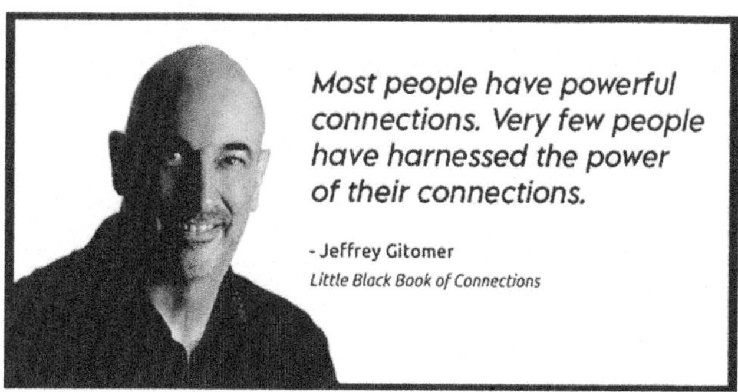

Survey For Success

One of the fastest and easiest ways to uncover opportunities for your practice is by sending out a Referability Survey to your patients, colleagues, and social sphere. Surveying your patients and professional network will help you:

- Spread the word about your practice
- Gain valuable insights into how people view you
- Capture testimonials you can use in your marketing
- Uncover opportunities to create profitable partnerships
- Generate referrals right on the spot

Best of all, a Referability Survey will help you achieve all of this quickly. In fact, you can send out your survey in as little as ten minutes.

Creating Your Referability Survey

The fastest and easiest way to survey your social sphere is using the survey tools in Facebook, LinkedIn, or wherever you have a social following. There are also some great free software tools to help you quickly and easily send a survey. JotForm.com and

Qualtrics.com allows you to survey your patients to capture ratings, reviews, and testimonials.

Creating a Referability Survey is as simple as asking people to rate you on a scale from 1-5 on how they view your:

- Trustworthiness
- Customer Service
- Quality of Work
- Professionalism
- Responsiveness

Sending a survey is super easy and only takes a few minutes. Follow the simple instructions, import or sync your contacts, and then select the specific people you want your survey sent to. Once your list is ready to go, customize your questions and message, then press send.

Your message can include the fact that your practice is in growth mode, so they know you are looking for additional patients. You can simply say something like:

> *"As one of my valued connections, I'd like to ask for your help. I'm working on growing my practice and have a quick survey I'd like you to complete. It's totally anonymous and should only take about 30 seconds.*

> *This will give me some important feedback, so I'd really appreciate it if you would take a moment to do it now."*

Then, for best results, add a thank you message that says,

> *"Thanks for sharing your feedback. Before you go, if some- one you know was asking about me or the care or services I provide, what would you tell them?"*

That last question is specifically designed to capture testimonials. Hopefully, you will get some great feedback and patient success stories or quotes you can use on your website and in your marketing collateral. You may even find people recommend or refer you right then and there because someone they know needs your services now.

Once your message says what you want, just press send, then sit back and watch the results roll in. If you send your survey to a large list, you should start seeing some completed surveys within minutes.

Value Your VIPs

You likely have some VIP patients who refer you regularly, and account for a large percentage of your overall revenue in your business. After coaching and consulting thousands of entrepreneurs and professionals over the years, I can tell you that the 80/20 rule is very real. What I mean is that for many people, 80% of their business comes from 20% of their clients and referral partners. These people should be treated like gold because they can represent tens or hundreds of thousands of dollars to your bottom line.

Having worked with dentists for over 15 years, Julieanne has had the pleasure of seeing how many dentists consistently receive the bulk of their patients through a few specific referral sources. Although they frequently utilize numerous forms of advertising and test countless tools designed to attract patients, the bulk of their new patients still continually get referred by reliable referral partners. She is no different as she has received most of her social media clients and coaching clients, from a couple of key referral sources. Primarily other dentists but also dental coaches, dental supply companies and web companies who know her well.

Take a moment to think about your practice. Over the past year, who has referred you the most business or the best patients? Do you have some past patients who refer to you more than others? If so, make sure you show them some appreciation.

Thank and Update Your Referral Champions

When people refer you, be sure to communicate with your patients or referral source partners throughout the process so they are always up to date. It's better to over-communicate rather than leave them wondering what's going on.

I learned this lesson back in 2005 after receiving a mortgage refinance referral from John Jones, a Vice President at Intel. John was definitely a VIP client. I helped him finance and then later refinance his primary home, as well as a vacation home he acquired. In addition to the thousands of dollars in commissions I earned from serving him personally, he regularly referred other Intel employees and executives to me. That's where I made one of my all-time biggest business blunders.

A couple of months after referring one of his colleagues to me, John asked how things had gone with his associate. Excitedly I said something like, *"Just great. We closed on his loan two weeks ago, so he is a happy camper."* To which he replied, *"Let me give you a tip. When someone refers business to you, it's a really good idea to follow up with the person and let them know what happened."*

My stomach dropped, and I felt like a total idiot. I couldn't believe I had been so dumb as to not update my VIP on the status of the client he had referred to me. If the referral had come from one of my referral partners, I absolutely would have kept them updated, but because it came from a client, the thought never even crossed my mind.

Needless to say, I apologized profusely and thanked him for the lesson. Then I quickly printed branded thank you cards with my company logo and a "thank you for your referral" message on the front with a pre-written message and blank line inside to fill in the name of the client they had referred. We quickly trained our thirty loan officers to send these out every time they received a referral from anyone. Our goal was to thank them for the referral, so they felt the love. We also made sure our team kept them updated throughout the entirety of the transaction.

In the years since, I've asked thousands of professionals if they've ever given a referral to someone and never heard back from the person to which they referred their clients. Unfortunately, nearly 100% of the people I've surveyed have had that same experience.

It doesn't take long to make a quick call or even just send an update by text or direct message. Alerting the people who refer you business will make them grateful for the update in just a few seconds. This will lead them to view you as a dependable professional worthy of sending their clients, colleagues, family, and friends to.

Send Video Messages & GIFs

When it comes to following up with people, one of the best ways to make a great impression is by recording and sending them a personalized video message. When you do, people will see your smiling face and be impressed that you are connecting in a way they likely haven't seen before. This personal touch takes only a few seconds and is much more impactful than sending a text, email, or direct message through a social platform. Simply record a quick video on your cell phone and text it to them like you would with a photo. If you are connected to them on Facebook or LinkedIn, you can record your video right on the messaging app and send it over in seconds.

Another way to help your message stand out is to send them an animated or video GIF. These are entertaining, quick, and easy to send. Plus, they help you stand out and can make your contact smile or laugh, feeling emotions they rarely experience through a simple text message. If you've never sent a video GIF, just find the GIF icon in your text messaging app and search for an image that conveys the message you want to send. For example, if you want to send someone a Happy Birthday message, search the term "Birthday." Then review and select the video GIF you think would best express the emotion you want to convey. Your message will make a lasting impression that will help you stand out from the crowd and build relationships faster.

There are a few ways you can update your Referral Champions:

- Call and thank them once their referred party contacts you
- Send a thank you card naming the person they referred
- Text or email an update whether the person moves forward or not
- If appropriate, share a photo of the work you performed
- Post the patient's testimonial on social media, thanking and tagging your Referral Champion
- Send a thank you gift after the transaction has closed Call your Referral Champion after the transaction is complete, showing your appreciation, and asking if there is anyone else you can help

The amount of time, energy, and money you spend thanking your Referral Champions will vary based on your Lifetime Patient Value. If a patient only represents a few hundred dollars to you, a simple call or text will do. However, if the patient means thousands of dollars to your business, you may want to go the extra mile to make sure your Referral Champions feel celebrated and rewarded.

The First Is the Worst

Do you remember the first time you tried to ride a bicycle? If you are like me, it felt scary, and you had visions of a disastrous painful crash. Most likely, you had a parent or family member assure you they would hold onto you, and everything would be fine. So, you pushed past the fear, grabbed the handlebars tight, and got up on that seat to face your fate.

As you anxiously started pedaling, you pleaded with the person teaching you to not let go so you wouldn't fall and fail. They assured you everything would be fine, so you started your way down the street, sidewalk, or parking lot. After a few seconds, you started figuring out how to adjust your weight and balance the bike. One minute in, you had already learned the basics of riding a bike.

Then you had that joyous moment when you actually felt you were in control of the bike and would soon be racing down the street. For me, that was the moment I looked up to realize I was riding by myself, and no one was holding on to my bike any longer. That was the point when I over adjusted the handlebars and quickly crashed on the pavement. After realizing the pain of colliding with the concrete hurt far less than I imagined, I got up, dusted off my scraped knees, and got back up determined to win. Needless to say, every other time I got on a bike after that experience, I was more confident than the first time because I had learned what to do and what not to do.

The lesson here is that typically the first time you do anything will be the absolute worst you will ever be at performing that task. After doing something new for the first time, you get wiser and better because you will know what you did not know the first time. You will be more comfortable because you will have learned some tips and tricks to improve your performance the second time around.

> *"Growing your practice starts by having the courage to know that you are already capable and that anything you don't already know can be learned. Have confidence as this is ultimately what you'll be giving your patients. Take the leap of faith, and you'll quickly see just what's possible.*
>
> \- Dr. Athena Goodarzi, Faculty 4M Institute

When it comes to engaging your Referral Champions, you just need to TAKE ACTION and get started. Fail forward as John Maxwell would say. The faster you TAKE ACTION, the faster you will find success. Just give yourself grace knowing the first is the worst and that every time after will get better and better.

Engaging your social sphere is one of the best ways to attract more Raving Referrals.

The good news is we are going to teach you how to create a Raving Rewards program in the next chapter.

Scan this QR code or visit the link below for a few quick tips on maximizing engagement through video:
https://ravingreferrals.com/engage/

Chapter 7

Referral Rewards

Referral Rewards can help you create a culture of referrals and automatically ask your patients and social sphere to actively refer you.

If you're like most professionals, you're probably really good at referring other people, but feel a little uncomfortable asking for referrals yourself. By adding a well-designed Referral Rewards campaign to your business or practice, you can systematize the process of asking for referrals and create a culture where asking for referrals is strategically added into all your patient communications.

That's why Referral Rewards campaigns can be one of the fastest and easiest ways to attract more referrals from your patients and social sphere.

Just think about the success that companies like Dropbox and Uber have had building their brand as well as their business valuation simply by offering rewards to satisfied clients. Your goal is to incentivize others to share and promote your service with their friends, family, coworkers, and colleagues.

The truth is that as human beings, we are biologically wired to help other people. In fact, there's nothing more fulfilling than helping someone else. That's why people's sense of service is such a powerful motivator.

> There is a tiny part of the brain, the hypothalamus, that likes validation it registers pleasure in doing good and being regonized for it, and it's home to the need to belong to something greater than ourselves.
>
> This is the social drive for making referrals. Human beings are physiologically wired to make referrals. That's why so many business can grow and thrive by tapping this business-building strategy along.
>
> **- JOHN JANTSCH**
> *The Referral Engine*

While your patients want to help you, their real motivation is wanting to help the people they care about improve their lives. If they feel like you can help people they know, they will be happy to refer them to you.

While your patients want to help you, their real motivation is wanting to help the people they care about improve their lives. If they feel like you can help people they know, they will be happy to refer them to you.

Adding a Referral Rewards program to your practice helps you combine the satisfaction people get by helping you and their friends with an attractive reward or incentive for introducing their loved ones to you. This creates a powerful referral engine that can generate patients for years to come.

Designing Your Referral Rewards Program

When creating your Referral Rewards program, there are four things you will need to do, which include:

- Choose a Program Type
- Choose a Reward Type
- Promote Your Program
- Recognize and Reward Referrers

Let's walk through each of these steps so you can design the optimal program for your business.

1. Choose a Program Type

There are two main types of Referral Rewards programs you can choose from: Referral Contests and Refer-A-Friend programs.

Referral Contests – In referral contests, patients receive entries for each person they refer. This means the more referrals they give, the higher their probability to win. This strategy can produce the fastest results and highest return on investment as it creates a campaign with a deadline that can lead to immediate new patient opportunities. That said, you will need to make the prize attractive enough to get people to refer others, as they won't automatically receive a benefit for recommending your business.

Refer-A-Friend Program – In these campaigns, you simply reward patients each time they refer someone to your practice. This is basically like an affiliate program where you compensate people for promoting and referring new patients to your practice.

When designing your campaign, you need to consider:

- Do you want to reward patients for each referral they give you, or only when referrals turn into new patients?
- Do you want to hold a short-term campaign, or create an ongoing referral campaign where patients always receive rewards when they refer you?

Both campaign types can be highly effective at driving referral activity. You simply need to decide what type of campaign will work best for your practice. Either way, we will teach you how to promote and build buzz around your campaign.

2. Choose A Reward Type

The good news about running a Referral Rewards campaign is that your patients have a natural desire to refer. That means if they are satisfied with your care and feel it would be valuable to others, they are naturally inclined to recommend you in order to help the people they know.

When designing your campaign, you should choose a reward that is aligned with and relevant. Use your creativity and come up with something fun and exciting. We recommend brainstorming the campaign and rewards with your team, staff, or referral partners. This creates more energy and brings life to the program.

Creating a referral culture within your practice can make a big difference. If you involve everyone on your team in the program creation process, you will increase both buy-in and long-term participation by your team members. Especially when you track and reward them when they help drive in new referrals from your patients, community partners, or even their own personal social sphere.

Now, before we discuss recommendations for potential Referral Rewards, we have to give you a quick disclaimer. You MUST research and understand all regulatory restrictions your industry may have when it comes to rewarding people for referrals. While most industries have no state or federal regulations that prohibit you from offering rewards or incentives, there are definite restrictions and guidelines within dentistry specifically. That's why it's always a good idea to check with your attorney regarding compensation restrictions that may apply to you.

Now that I've given you our official disclaimer and made our attorneys happy, let's explore some great incentives to reward your Referral Champions.

Popular Referral Rewards Used in Many Industries:

- Cash Rewards
- Gift Certificates for your Services or Discounts
- Movie, Restaurant, or Starbucks Gift Cards
- iPads, Tablets, and TVs
- Tickets to Concerts or Sporting Events
- Inclusion in Special Patient Appreciation Parties
- Weekend Getaways or Mini-Vacations
- Related Products or Services Provided by your Referral Partners
- Reward system of points and having several options to choose from, based on points available

Your goal is to get people excited about referring to you, so they're constantly on the lookout scouting for your new patients. Of course, rewards that give away the products or services you provide are an easy and natural option. Plus, those who refer patients to you are already patients themselves and are more likely to use your service again anyway. That's why giving incentives for your service can help boost loyalty. In addition, promoting your service as the reward gives you another opportunity to remind people about what you offer.

How Much Should You Spend?

When deciding upon your Referral Reward, remember the money you invest in the campaign will be a fraction of the potential profit of all the new patients you are receiving. This is especially true when you consider the lifetime value of each new patient.

When offering cash or gift certificates as rewards to referral partners, you need to decide if you want to offer a flat fee reward, or a percentage of the purchases made. Both strategies work well, but your program should be aligned with your industry, business model, and brand. Sometimes reviewing referral ideas that other industries have found success in, can trigger great ideas for dentistry that fit within necessary guidelines.

For Example:

Refer 4 and It's Free – this gives patients a 25% credit or discount for future purchases. Of course, not all patients will redeem these rewards, which will mean you will have no expense for some of the referrals you receive, and your patients still feel good that they received a reward even if they never redeem it. The downside of this type of reward is that the tracking and accounting can be cumbersome.

$25 / $50 / $100 Referral Reward – this strategy is similar to the one we just discussed. The difference is that this allows you to give a physical gift certificate or gift card that patients can use in the future. People often feel more recognized and rewarded when receiving a physical gift in the mail. Plus, if a professional wins your contest or prize, it gives you a great reason to pop-by their place of business to deliver the prize in person and deepen your relationship.

10% Referral Reward – this strategy is more of an affiliate model where you incentivize people who refer you by sharing the revenues you generate with them. This strategy can be highly successful but should be used with strategic alliances and referral partners rather than patients, as some people may feel uncomfortable being paid for helping people they care about.

3. Promote Your Program

Now that you've decided upon the type of campaign and reward that is best for your business, it's time to start promoting it.

When creating your referral program, make it as easy as possible for people to refer clients to you. That's why we suggest you incorporate the following promotional strategies:

- **Print referral cards:** You can actually empower your patients with printed referral cards that give their friends discounts or special offers. Consider incorporating a discount or reward for your patients when they refer their friends, so both people have extra motivation to take advantage of your offer and use your services. Just be sure to train your staff to give these out to all of your patients.
- **Give out gift certificates:** Giving gift certificates is another way you can empower your patients to spread the word about your business. If you decide to give out gift certificates, be sure to include a brochure on services to make it easier for people to share why they love your practice.
- **Post signs in your practice:** Print a sign you display on your front desk, reception area, and other public areas.
- **Mail your best patients:** To announce your program, send out a personal letter or thank you card to each of your best patients. You may want to ask them for their help in referring their friends or simply thank them for their business and give them a way to help their loved ones. Either way, sending them a friendly letter person- ally signed by you along with gift certificates or referral cards they can give to their friends can help boost your business quickly.
- **Incorporate throughout your business:** Another easy way to promote your new Referral Rewards program is to incorporate your offer into your invoices, receipts, and other statements. Look at each and every printed or electronic communication you send to your patients throughout your patient engagement cycle and look for ways to promote your program. You can also include your referral cards or gift certificates in anything you mail, ship, or deliver to your patients. That way, you are automatically asking for referrals without ever having to ask yourself.
- **Call your best patient:** You should also consider calling your most pleasurable or profitable patients and letting them know you want to do something special for them. By making a personal call, you deepen your relationship and

create an opportunity for your patients to give you referrals immediately during your call.

- **Create a video:** Shoot a quick 1-or 2-minute video giving the details of your Referral Rewards campaign. Post the video on YouTube and include a link on your website, newsletter, and all your social media sites.
- **Email your sphere:** Once you are ready to promote your program, be sure to email your database of patients and potential referral partners with details about your referral campaign or contest. You may even want to include a private offer to a special that is exclusively available to friends and family of your best patients. This helps people feel special and increase the likelihood they will pass on your promotion to their family and friends.
- **Go social:** Promote your campaign or contest on your social media sites and fan pages, including Facebook, LinkedIn, Google+, Instagram, and Twitter.

You can share the Referral Reward you are offering to incentivize your social sphere to spread the word. This helps expand your reach beyond your current patient base to maximize the awareness for your campaign.

- **Promote on your website:** Be sure to include an announcement on the homepage of your website along with your blogs. Remember to give people plenty of reasons to spread the word and include links to your special offer and appointment or calendar link.
- **Announce in your newsletter:** Include a Referral Rewards section in your printed or electronic newsletter. Since you are already promoting your business and educating your patients, newsletters give you a natural opportunity to ask for referrals and promote the rewards you are offering to those who do. As we will discuss in the next section, you should also recognize and thank referring patients.

- **Promote with your partners:** To increase the total exposure of your campaign, we recommend including your referral partners. You can either design the program jointly with some of your best partners or simply give them referral cards or gift certificates they can give to their clients. This helps them feel good because it helps them increase their perceived value with their clients. This also enrolls them with an easy means of recommending you when the opportunity presents itself.

When creating your campaign promotion, remember to:

- **Use photos showing your rewards:** An attractive photo of the reward you are offering will help build buzz and entice people to refer you. If you're giving away a gift certificate or gift card, be sure to print the value of the gift card in text over the photo showing the product or service people will receive.
- **Include entry and reward/prize info:** If you are holding a referral contest, be sure to give detailed descriptions of your prize as well as a description of how people earn entries in your contest. Be sure to include all of the rules or restrictions of your campaign. If you are promoting your contest online, include a link to a rules page or list them on the bottom of your Referral Rewards page.

Include share buttons and social media links: This makes it easy for people to recommend you to their friends and social sphere. If you are promoting your program online, you want to take advantage of the network reach of social media by incorporating a share button on your website, Instagram, or Facebook page. You may also want to give your patients suggestions of how they can best recommend you to other people.

Always Be Promoting

However you choose to promote your Referral Rewards pro- gram, the key to your success will be the amount of promotion you do and just how creative you get with it. In our age of information overload, attention spans have never been shorter. If you send out a single email, post, or tweet about your program, that won't be enough to keep people engaged with your program. You don't want to annoy your patients, but you should send subtle reminders periodically to keep your Referral Rewards program top of mind. Consistency is the key.

Whatever method you choose, remember that effective promotion of your patient referral program is an ongoing process. If you want your program to be successful, you need to remind people about it from time to time. Keep people engaged with your program through regular emails and social posts online, and not only will you bring in new patients but also more passionate fans that compound your referrals exponentially.

4. Recognize and Reward Referrers

Throughout your Referral Rewards campaign, you should be recognizing and rewarding anyone who refers others to you. This is actually the best way to continually promote your program. Not only will you show your patients how grateful you are for their referrals, but you are also triggering their ego-based need for recognition. As you illustrate examples of patients who are referring their friends, you build social proof and help others feel more comfortable and more likely to refer you. Just be sure to request permission in writing from patients if you are going to be acknowledging them by name publicly so you stay compliant with all HIPAA laws and regulations.

You can use each of the promotional strategies we covered in the last section to promote your top referrers. You may even want to create a referral leader board where you prominently recognize people who are referring new business. Again, this helps ensure your entire team or organization is active in the Referral Rewards campaign and conversation.

If you are holding a referral contest, be sure to recognize referrers throughout your contest. This helps build buzz and keeps the campaign alive. At the conclusion of your referral contest, be sure to recognize the winner(s).

For optimal results, we recommend that you:

- Shoot a video or go live on social media showing the drawing of the winning name to create excitement and show the drawing Is being held fairly.
- Send an email to your email list congratulating the winner(s). We recommend you list the names of every single person who referred new patients to you as they will appreciate the recognition. This is often a stronger motivator than any prize you may offer. Be sure to include your referral partners as this is a great opportunity to promote them and their business to your patient base.
- Post on all of your websites, social media sites, and fan pages to get extra mileage out of the campaign.
- Ask the winner to give you a shout-out on their social media pages and create a quick thank you video.
- Email contestants offering them an alternative prize which may be a gift certificate or discount on your services.
- Meet with the winner to give them their prize in person. Take a photo or video showing the referral partner receiving their prize. This will allow you to promote it in your office, on your website, social media, and in other communications.
- If your services are part of the prize, capture the winner's testimonial and ask them for referrals to people who fit your ideal patient profile. Video is best because you can transcribe it and use it in print as well.

Following these steps will help you create a powerful and profitable referral contest. Once your contest ends, consider promoting another contest or event to keep the momentum building and to prime patients for future campaigns.

As you can see, creating a Referral Rewards campaign can create tremendous word-of-mouth recommendations and referrals for your business. By incorporating these practices into your business, you create a culture of referrals quickly and easily. Doing so will help you eliminate your high-cost marketing activities while providing you with a steady stream of ideal patients.

Here are some examples showing how some people recognize their referral contest winners:

While one of the best ways to motivate can be to compensate there are other ways to do this, if necessary, given any industry restrictions.

Recognizing and rewarding your Referral Champions can boost your business quickly. Get people scouting business for you by scanning this QR code or visiting the following link:

https://ravingreferrals.com/reward

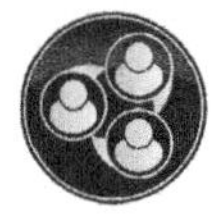

Chapter 8

Master the Art of the Ask

The number one reason some dentists receive more referrals than others is that they simply ask for them. Many people feel uncomfortable and awkward asking their patients for referrals. However, once you are prepared and you have a strategy for when and how to ask, it will feel natural and comfortable for you, your staff, and your patients.

In their book Selling Professional Services, Chuck and Evan Polin write,

> *"Most professionals do not ask of referrals because they are afraid they have nothing to offer in return. They are often surprised when they discover that the referring party's only expectation is that their client or friend receive the best service. When you ask for referrals, the other party typically expects less in return than you would think."*

Set the Stage

While some dentists have their teams ask for referrals once they have finished serving their patients, we recommend having a conversation about referrals and introductions at the end of your first patient consultation. This sets the stage for a referral conversation later.

Earl Kemper is a referral master and has been recognized as the #1 coach for ActionCOACH five times for the Americas region and twice globally. Earl is truly skilled at helping companies grow and create predictable profitability. A cornerstone of Earl's system is the ability to grow the business by systemizing their referrals.

Earl primarily coaches top-producing financial advisors helping them dramatically increase assets under management. He teaches them to weave a pre-referral request into every new patient conversation saying:

> *"Thanks so much for meeting with me today. Before you leave, I'd like to ask for your help. As you may know, I am in the process of expanding my business, and one of the ways I keep my costs down is by working primarily by referral, so I don't have to spend much time or money on advertising. Once I've taken care of you and hopefully have exceeded your expectations, I'd like to ask your permission to ask you for referrals. Would that be all right?"*

You'll find people are extremely receptive to this question because everyone likes to help other people. Also, you haven't asked them for a referral at that moment in time. You've simply gotten their permission to ask them for referrals and introductions in the future once you've provided your services and earned their trust.

Listen for Referral Triggers

After your patient has given their approval to ask for referrals and introductions in the future, you need to be on the lookout for expressions of appreciation. These Referral Triggers let you know when it's time to ask for a referral or introduction because your patients are in peak referral state.

Listen closely, and whenever your patients say any of these Referral Triggers, it's time to ask for referrals:

- Thank you so much!
- I love my new smile!
- This was so much easier/faster than I expected!
- You are so good at what you do!
- You're the best!
- This is beautiful!
- I love your staff. Everyone here is so friendly!
- I look/feel great!
- My mom/brother/sister/friend/neighbor/coworker
- needs to have some dental work done.
- I have a friend/neighbor/patient who is looking for a new dentist.
- I should introduce you to…

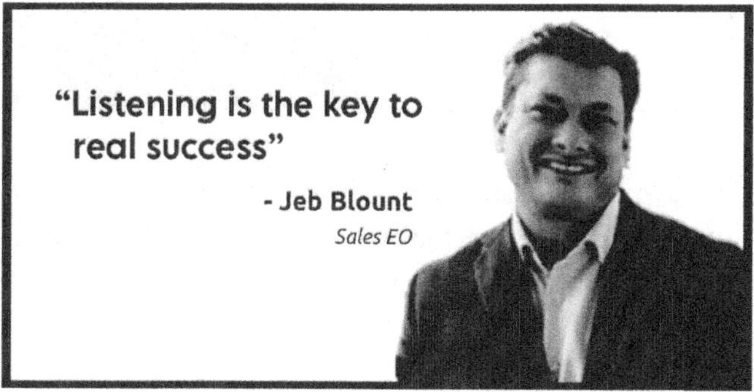

When you hear any of these Referral Triggers, immediately smile and say,

> *"I'm so glad you feel that way. I love helping patients like you {share your Service Statement}. By the way,*

I may have mentioned before that we are expanding our practice, so if you know any {describe your Perfect Patient} who might need help {share your Service Statement}, we'd love to offer them a free consultation and would even be willing to give them free x-rays since they are a referral from you.

Do you know anyone right now who is looking for a new dentist?"

Be ready to ask for referrals when opportunities arise and when trust has been established in the relationship. Actively listen for the Referral Triggers and be prepared to deliver your ***ask*** confidently and naturally.

Never miss a prime opportunity to ask. Even if they don't have a referral for you now, you've planted a seed and set the stage so they refer you later when they hear of someone that might benefit from your care.

What you'll find is that when people voluntarily express their appreciation for your work, they are much more likely to introduce you to others who need your services. Plus, you get the added benefit of your perfect prospects hearing a passionate testimonial about you and the services you provide.

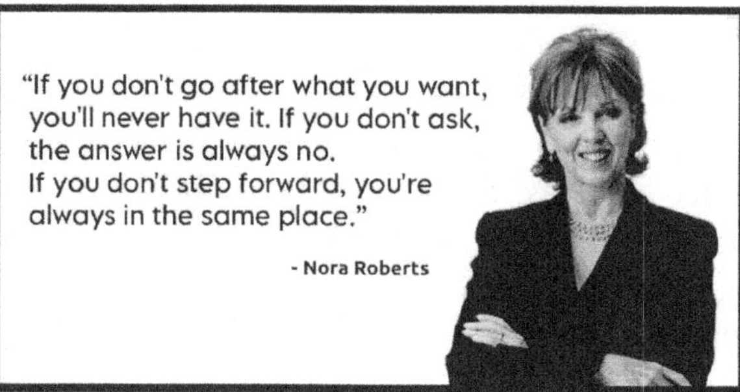

A-S-K to G-E-T

One of the greatest lessons I've learned from Mark Victor Hansen is to A-S-K to G-E-T. If you've never read his book with Jack Canfield called, *The Aladdin Factor*, take a moment and order it now either in printed form, eBook, or as an audiobook. The key concept of the book is that the more you ask for what you want, the more you will get it.

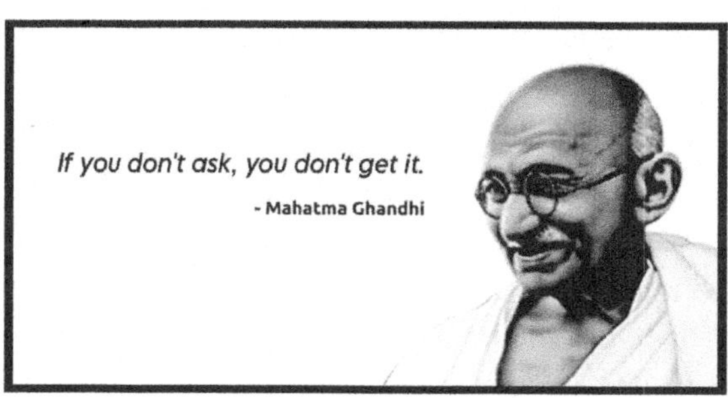

By asking patients questions about their satisfaction with your care, you set the stage for an expression of appreciation which often leads to opportunities to ask for referrals.

When meeting with your patients, try inserting the following questions into the conversation:

- I hope you're pleased with the outcome. Is there anything I can do to make you even happier?

- Now that you've been my patient for a while, I'm wondering if you can tell me what you have found most valuable about our practice?
- I'm committed to growing my practice through exceptional service. On a scale of 1-10, how happy would you say you are with our practice? What would make it a 10?
- Do you mind if I ask what you have liked best about being a patient at our practice?
- If you don't mind me asking, if you knew someone who was looking for a new dental home, how likely would you be to recommend me? What would you say?

If the patient responds positively, you can follow up by saying,

> *"I'm so glad to hear that. I hope you'll recommend me any time you hear anyone mention they are looking for a good dentist, are experiencing tooth pain or just want to improve their smile. Anyone come to mind?"*

Not only will these questions lead to more referrals, but they will also give you testimonials you can use to market your ser- vices. Just be sure to capture what they say and ask for permission to use their testimonial on your website and promotional materials.

Another way for you to comfortably ask for referrals is by saying:

> *"By the way, if you ever have a friend or family member you think might benefit from my services, I would be happy to offer them a free consultation and free x-rays."*

Ideally, you should describe your *Perfect Patient Profile* and *Service Statement*, so they know exactly what type of patients you are looking to serve and how you help them. You might simply say that one of your specialties is working with moms with busy schedules or whatever describes your perfect patient. Adding this detail into the conversation gives them clarity so they will be on the lookout for patients they can refer you.

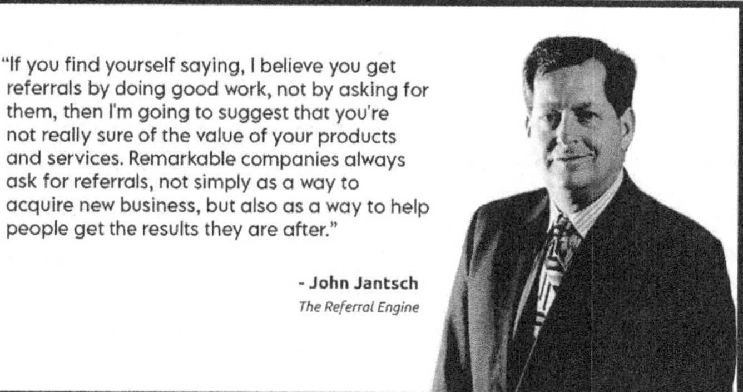

Referral Offers and Discounts

Another way you can comfortably ask for referrals and introductions is by letting patients know you offer special services, offers, or discounts for referred patients. You might say something like:

> *"As you may know, I love working with people who are referred to us. Right now, we're giving a special discount to friends or family of our existing patients. If there's anyone you'd like to refer, they will get an extra 20% off our any treatment they need. And, of course, I'll take extra special care of them since they're coming from you. Is there anyone you can think of who might like to take advantage of this?"*

For optimal results, we suggest creating and giving them a refer-a-friend gift certificate they can quickly and easily hand out to people when they talk about your services. This gives prospective patients an overview of your services, along with a testimonial from someone they trust.

As you start integrating these conversations into your patient dialogues, you will find people are happy to refer others when asked at the right time and in the right way.

Larry Stites, co-founder of Allure Dental Studio says,

> *"Have the courage to ask the tough questions. Set aside your fears of being judged or rejected and pursue your dreams with hard work and determination. Not doing so leads to a life only imagined in your own mind and a life that never reached full potential."*

Practice and Perfect

While you've probably spent thousands of hours practicing and perfecting your trade or profession, you most likely haven't spent much time learning and practicing how to attract referrals and introductions. Since practice makes perfect, we recommend you partner with another professional and role-play these conversations, so they become second nature to you both.

As you master the art of the ask, you will find that patients refer you without even being asked as you build a business that is powered by referrals. In addition to asking for referrals, start asking for anything and everything you want in life.

- Ask for an appointment
- Ask for an introduction
- Ask to take the next step
- Ask if you can give them a tour
- Ask if they would like to move forward

Asking for what you want dramatically increases the likelihood that you will get it. Best of all, you have nothing to lose because if the answer is no, you are in the exact same position you were before you asked. If they say yes, you will have achieved your desired outcome and have moved your business forward.

Mastering the Art of the Ask is one of the top practices that create more success. Scan the QR code or visit the link below for a quick video message on how to A-S-K and G-E-T. While we're on the subject, we're asking you to share this video with your network. Together, we can help them get clear on what they are asking for in their personal and professional lives:

https://RavingReferrals.com/ask

Chapter 9

Patient Appreciation Events

Back in 1999, I learned the value of appreciation parties from a Realtor named Mikalan Moiso. Each year, she held her annual New Year's Eve party at a swanky downtown hotel in Portland, Oregon. It was the event of the year, and in order to get an invitation to the black-tie event, you simply had to give Mikalan at least one good referral throughout the course of the year.

My wife and I will never forget ringing in the new millennium of 2000 playing poker, listening to the Frank Sinatra crooner, and tasting delicious eats and treats.

Months after the event, I asked Mikalan how impactful the event was on her business. I was shocked to hear that her annual event is the single biggest source of clients for her. In fact, she had shifted the vast majority of her annual marketing budget to the event because her clients and social sphere wanted to make sure they gave her referrals, so they received their golden ticket to the event. The event was so successful, it led to Mikalan being named the 2004 Portland Metropolitan Association of Realtors® Broker of the Year.

After learning this strategy from her, I went on to host several client appreciation events, including private concerts, movie showings, wine tastings, holiday parties, and charity events.

Everyone loves a great party. That's why a great way to show your patients how much they mean to your business is to throw a patient appreciation party. A patient event can be an impactful way to celebrate your patients, recognize milestones, and say "thank-you" for all the business they have referred to you and your practice. Not only will you bring patients together for a fun and festive event, but you also create a culture of community that unites your team as you create an evening your patients will never forget.

- Art Showings – Partner with an art gallery and host a private showing.
- Awards Parties – Invite your patients to a hotel, bar, restaurant, or private theater to watch the Oscars, Grammys, Golden Globes, or other awards show.
- Bowling Parties – Rent an entire bowling alley or just a few lanes and give prizes for the bowlers who get the most strikes or spares as well as the top individual and team scores.
- Casino Night – Hire a party company to bring casino tables and dealers giving out chips and awarding prizes for the top chip stacks.
- Charity Fundraising Events – Create your own event or buy a table at a fundraising dinner inviting your top patients, referral partners or even reps.
- Concerts – Buy tickets for your VIP patients or partners to an upcoming concert or host a private party with an 80s cover band or local musician.
- Cornhole Tournaments – Host a cornhole tournament inviting top patients to register their own teams.
- Golf Tournaments – Produce your own golf tournament or simply buy a foursome and invite VIPs to join you on the greens.
- Holiday Parties – Throw a private party for Valentine's Day, Independence Day, Halloween, Thanksgiving, Christmas, or New Year's Eve.

- Private Movie Showings – Rent out a theater and have your own private showing of the latest blockbuster film.
- Sports Events – Host a tailgate party, rent a private box, or simply buy tickets and invite your best patients for a sporting event.
- TopGolf Tournaments – Rent a few private bays at TopGolf and give prizes for top scores.
- Wine Tours and Tastings – Host a private party at a winery or tasting room.

Become a Charity Champion

Of all the events and campaigns that I've used over the years, the most fulfilling and rewarding have been charity events. In my opinion, one of the absolute best ways to build goodwill with your patients is to support charities and causes you are passionate about.

Cause-related marketing has evolved from a short-term tactic used to spike sales into a powerful positioning discipline used to build brand equity and elevate corporate perception. It's not only good for the community; it's good for business.

A great example of being a Charity Champion is what Dr. Sam and Randa Bollwinkel are doing with their charity, Community of Smiles Outreach (COSO). As dentists, Sam and Randa saw first-hand the impact a smile could have on the self-confidence and overall health of a patient. That led them to start their own charity with a mission to provide access to comprehensive dental care to people with limited or no dental insurance coverage—specifically those whose dental needs impact their smile.

What sets them apart is that COSO focuses on providing care for employees, volunteers, and beneficiaries of community-based nonprofits. Through partnerships with 3D Infusion Institute which provides postgraduate dental training, and dental equipment manufacturers, patients receive care from experienced dentists using some of the latest technologies available.

Sam and Randa's long-term goal is to build a sustainable and replicable model that will impact communities around the world. COSO provides opportunities for philanthropists, granting organizations, and corporate donors to make life-changing differences in the lives of individuals and their families.

The Results Are In

There have been numerous research studies over the years that prove consumers want to know about the impact your company or practice makes in their community and in the world. The more you communicate what you are doing to make a difference, the more loyalty you win with your patients.

Just take a look at what research companies have learned after surveying Americans nationwide:

- 83% of U.S. consumers want more of the products and services they use to benefit causes.
- 80% said they'd be "likely to switch brands, about equal in price and quality, to one that supports a cause".
- 93% of consumers want to know what companies are doing to make the world a better place.
- 66% of people believe it's no longer enough for corporations to merely give money away, but that they must integrate good causes into their day-to-day business.
- 90% of consumers want companies to tell them the ways they are supporting causes.

While this research is a few years old, we believe this is a trend that will continue to grow. Especially with Millennials and Generation Z having been raised in this new era of corporate responsibility and social impact. Bottom line, the more you show you care, the more you inspire your community to care about you and your company. So, choose a charity or cause that you are passionate about that is in alignment with your brand and your community. Get involved and design ways that your practice and your community can make a difference – together.

The Ultimate Wishman

One of the favorite people I've had the pleasure of meeting was Frank Shankwitz, co-founder of the Make-A-Wish Foundation. Changing lives and granting wishes is what Frank dedicated his life to. If you haven't seen the movie *Wishman* about Frank's life, you owe it to yourself to watch this heartwarming film. You'll be glad you did.

While serving as an Arizona Highway Patrol officer, Frank had the honor of granting a wish for a 7-year-old boy named Chris who was battling leukemia. Turned out this boy had a dream of being a Highway Patrol Motorcycle Officer like his heroes, Ponch and John, from the television show, "CHiPs". After hearing of Chris' desire, Frank and a few of his fellow officers sprang into action and made Chris' dream come true.

They had a uniform custom-crafted for Chris and gave him an old police badge and a "Smokey Bear" hat so he would feel like a real cop. Frank even set up a special course so Chris could drive a battery-powered motorcycle and qualify for the officer's wings he so deeply desired. A few short days later, Chris' body gave up the fight, and on May 3, 1980, he passed away.

This event led Frank to found Make-A-Wish to grant wishes for other sick children. Not long ago, I asked Frank what helped the charity become the global force for the good that it is today. Frank's answer was simple and powerful, "Disneyland." Turns out the first official wish the start-up charity granted was taking 7-year-old Frank 'Bopsy' Salazar to Disneyland.

This powerful partnership created massive visibility for both organizations and inspired millions of people to donate and do more for others in need. What started as a simple way to help a dying boy fulfill his wish, has led to over 450,000 children having their dreams fulfilled.

Over the years, Disney has invested millions of dollars promoting the impact they have made by granting wishes for Make-A-Wish kids. Every time a mom watches a commercial or story of a dying child's wish being fulfilled at Disneyland, it boosts loyalty and wins Disney another fan of the brand.

Starting Small Makes a Big Difference

The good news is that you don't have to create your own charity to tap into the power of cause-related marketing. You can simply raise awareness, funds, and support for great causes and charities already doing good work.

If you're curious how I got started as a Charity Champion, you're going to love the next chapter.

Everyone loves to have fun. That's why patient appreciation events are a great way to recognize and reward your best patients and referral partners.

Scan this QR code or visit the link below
for a quick video message on how to
grow your business celebrating your community:

https://ravingreferrals.com/celebrate/

Chapter 10

Referral of a Lifetime

My favorite referral of all time was to Mark Victor Hansen, co-author of the best-selling book series Chicken Soup for the Soul. Mark is an amazing man who has appeared on *Oprah, CNN,* and *The Today Show,* as well as in *Time Magazine, U.S. News & World Report, USA Today, The New York Times,* and *Entrepreneur Magazine.*

Among Mark's many achievements is his Guinness book world record for selling the most non-fiction books in the history of the world, with over 500 million books sold. That's a staggering number that still blows my mind.

I was referred to Mark by one of his closest friends back in 2004 when I was serving as a volunteer on the Corporate Industry Council for the charity Northwest Medical Teams, which has since rebranded to Medical Teams International (MedicalTeams.org). This faith-based charity provides emergency medical relief in response to floods, famine, and other natural disasters.

I got involved after hearing one of their volunteer doctors share his story of taking what I call a voluntour trip over to Africa. The doctor recounted his story of 18-hour days spent caring for countless patients. No matter how many patients he treated, each day ended with a mother chasing the van crying, *"What about my child?"* The doctor's heartbreaking story stirred my heart into action, so I accepted the invitation and started raising money and awareness for the work they were doing.

The Perfect Choice

The biggest fundraiser of the year for Northwest Medical Teams was their annual *Spirit of Life Awards*, where they would honor a local titan of business for their impact on the community.

Knowing I was a fan of personal development training, I was asked to help secure the featured speaker for the luncheon. Having just read, *The One Minute Millionaire, The Enlightened Way to Wealth* by Mark Victor Hansen and Robert Allen, I knew their message of doing well by doing good would be a perfect fit for this audience and encourage the attendees to give more.

As fortune would have it, a financial advisor friend named Al Sizer had known Mark for over 30 years. It turns out Mark and Al came up together on the public speaking circuit back in the 1970s and had built a special friendship forged over three decades of traveling together and speaking at the same events.

After working up the courage to ask Al to ask Mark to speak at the event, I was beyond excited when Al called back, saying Mark's calendar was available that day and he was interested in helping.

After learning Mark's speaking fee, it was clear the charity couldn't afford him. After all, any fee NW Med paid would reduce the total impact the charity made, which was the entire reason for the event. That's when I made the courageous step of covering Mark's speaker fee myself. Fortune favors the bold, so I gave my financial commitment and took a deep breath of faith, knowing that paying it forward always has a high ROI.

Two for the Price of One

What happened next was amazing. When coordinating the details with Mary, Mark's Vice President, she was so inspired by the cause we were supporting that she generously offered to have Mark speak in the evening at no additional cost in addition to the lunch event. This meant we were able to put on two events while he was in town.

Again, I said YES and quickly went to work producing an additional evening event we called "*Success with Integrity*," with my company, Integrity Lending, as the event's premier sponsor. This empowered my loan officers to invite their top clients and referral partners to join us for this fun, feel-good, celebrity event. I have to tell you, the pride and unity this event brought to my team was immeasurable and was celebrated for months.

The morning of May 18, 2004, I had the honor of joining Mark Victor Hansen and Al Sizer for breakfast, along with three representatives of NW Med, including the CEO and the Chairman of the board, as well as the development director I had been working with for months.

During our breakfast, Mark asked about my companies and nonchalantly shared, *"I can easily refer you a billion dollars in commercial loans,"* at which point quick calculations of the commissions and income that represented flashed through my head. That was the moment it hit me just how influential this man was and how impactful his endorsement could be for both my companies and me personally.

Throughout the day, Mark inspired and entertained over 500 people, helping us raise donations that delivered over $1.2 million worth of medical aid and supplies to those in need. As you can imagine, it was a day I will never forget.

As he closed his final presentation of the night, Mark made an offer for those who wanted to learn more. I immediately went to the back of the room and bought every CD and book he had for sale, including *Dreams Don't Have Deadlines, The Power of Focus*, and *The Aladdin Factor – How to Ask for and Get Anything You Want.*

The following week, as my wife and I traveled to Maui, I spent much of the trip listening to Mark mentor me through his audios. Mark's masterful training expanded my thinking and helped me reframe what was possible for my life.

During each of Mark's talks, he challenged the audience to make a list of 101 goals, including the date each person planned to achieve each goal they set. Since my wife goes to bed early, I spent hours every night on the beach under the stars dreaming of all I hoped to achieve over my lifetime. By the end, I had created hundreds of short and long-term goals.

One of my top ambitions was to enroll Mark Victor Hansen to become my personal mentor. After returning from Maui, I gathered my nerve and made what felt like the scariest call I had ever made, asking Mark to be my personal mentor. He graciously agreed and has impacted my life in countless ways since I stepped out in faith and asked for what I wanted.

Mark had no idea, but one of the goals I wrote on that beach was, *"To have Mark Victor Hansen write about me in a book by May 28, 2005."* A few months after writing down that goal, Mark called and said, *"Robert Allen and I are writing our follow-up to The One Minute Millionaire which will be called Cracking the Millionaire Code. We'd like to feature you in the book. Would you be okay with that?"*

Excitedly, I said *"YES,"* and almost as if by divine design, *Cracking the Millionaire Code* was published on May 31, 2005. Just three days after the goal date I had set one year earlier.

Dreams Fulfilled

Within 12 months of following Mark's system and writing down my goals, I had traveled to Asia, Europe, Africa, and South America for business. These were foreign lands I had only dreamt of traveling to before soaking in Mark's mentorship.

Before meeting Mark, the largest transaction I had been involved with was a $10 million development loan. Now, I was working on international financings of $200 million. Twenty times larger than any transaction I had been involved in before Mark telling the world about me!

You can just imagine the clients and opportunities that the book brought because of the credibility and social proof of Mark's endorsement and promotion. When a celebrity or company with massive authority and influence endorses and promotes you, it creates tremendous credibility that unlocks lucrative opportunities.

Within weeks of writing out my goals, Mark invited me to be a VIP guest of his MEGA Book Marketing, MEGA Info-Marketing, and MEGA Speaking Empire conferences. He routinely had me stand and introduce myself and share how I could help the audience. He later asked me to teach finance to his Enlightened Millionaire Institute Inner Circle both in the U.S. and abroad.

Around the World in 30 Days

That book became a turning point in my career, not only because of the business opportunities that came from readers of the book, but more importantly because the experience was powerful proof of our human ability to create and manifest anything we want. The key is to get clear on exactly what we want to achieve, accomplish, or experience.

Of the 338 goals I wrote on that beach, over 100 were achieved in the first 12 months alone, a few of which included:

- Enroll Mark Victor Hansen as my personal mentor by 7/7/2004
- Have Mark Victor Hansen write about me in a book published by 5/28/2005
- Have Mark Victor Hansen invite me to his private home in Kona, Hawaii, by 5/28/2005
- Start a 501(c)3 charity by 5/28/2005
- Travel to New York City, London, Hong Kong, China, and Africa by 5/28/2005
- Hike the Great Wall of China by 5/28/2005
- Meet U2's lead singer Bono by 5/28/2005

Prior to meeting Mark, I had barely left the country. Within one year of his mentoring, I took a 30-day around-the-world trip Eastward from Portland, Oregon to London, then off to Hong Kong, Macau, and Guangzhou, China, before taking the final leg to Caracas, Venezuela and Bucaramunga, Colombia.

As I met new clients and prospective partners, I gave them a copy of the Cracking the Millionaire Code book with my business card inserted on the page that started featuring my personal, professional, and charitable pursuits. That book elevated my status with my clients, team, and referral partners while simultaneously attracting new clients from around the world – just as Mark had predicted.

Mark taught me the power of specificity in goal setting, including writing down the exact date you plan to achieve each goal. In case you missed it, Cracking the Millionaire Code was published three days after the goal date I had typed on my laptop less than one year prior, a fact that astounds me to this day.

My purpose in sharing this story with you is two-fold.

First, I want you to truly understand that you can create anything you want in your life when you get clear, put it in writing, and commit yourself to achieve your desire or dream. You will have to take massive action and ask others to assist you, but you can quickly transform your life simply by transforming your thinking.

Second, I hope to give you a vision for the power of getting endorsed, recommended, and promoted by people and companies that have the ability to take your business to an entirely new level. The key takeaway here is that just one key referral partner can transform your business and your life.

You just have to A-S-K to G-E-T.

Getting clear on what you want to achieve, and experience is the foundation of success.

Scan this QR code or visit the link below for an inspiring lesson on setting the goals that matter most to your future success:

https://ravingreferrals.com/mvh/

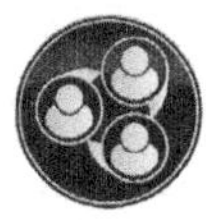

Chapter 11

Wealth Through Workshops for Specialty Dentists

After meeting and being mentored by Mark Victor Hansen, one of the most important lessons he taught me was the power of producing events. It can be one of the single most effective ways to boost your expert status and book consults by educating audiences in person or online.

> *"It is important that dental professionals share their knowledge and experience by educating others. In doing so, they are providing an invaluable service for their colleagues (and, ultimately, patients.) In the process, the dental professional becomes a respected source of information and thought leadership, and naturally gains respect and recognition from peers, patients, and other professionals. This recognition paves the way for even more opportunities for success and growth. Ultimately, becoming a speaking and consulting influencer will generate a solid platform for professional growth."*
>
> *Vanessa Emerson*
> *Founder of The Dental Speaker & Dental Speaker Institute*

If you're a dental specialist, holding educational workshops is one of the best ways to win new referring offices. Events help you attract highly profitable prospects and establish yourself as a credible expert, which, in turn, will help you attract and retain more referring practices at higher conversion rates.

The key is to fill your workshops with as many of your perfect referring dental practices as possible so that you maximize the revenue you generate for your business. Events can be held for potential patients direct to the public as well.

When it comes to holding educational events, quality trumps quantity every time. It is better to teach a class to 10 practice owners or 10 potential high-quality patients who match your Perfect Prospect Profile than to have 100 unqualified people in your audience. Be sure your event invitations and promotions are targeted to appeal to your ideal patients or referring partners. Consider implant study clubs, collaborative treatment planning, or even an event titled, "Why don't I restore those teeth?" etc. In the case of direct-to-consumer events, you might consider teaching about what is possible with a smile makeover along with the long-term benefits, as an example. For the purpose of this section, we will focus on events for referring practices with our examples.

7 Super Strategies to Fill Your Events with Perfect Prospects

The following seven time-tested and proven strategies will help you fill your next event with quality candidates for your services:

1. Invite Your Social Sphere

The best way to fill your events is with your current referring practices. They are the most likely to use your services again! In addition to your referring practices, you should also promote your upcoming events to both your personal and professional databases. Since these people already know, like, and trust you, they are likely to recommend your event once you have asked for their help and identified who the event will be most helpful for. If you charge for your events, you may want to offer a few gift guest passes people can give to their friends, clients, and colleagues. Just be sure to identify your perfect prospect profile, so they invite the right type of people to your event.

Here are a few ways you can invite hundreds of prospects in a matter of minutes:

- Email flyers and invitations to family, friends, and dentists in your local area.
- Post events in your social network through Facebook, Twitter, Google+, and LinkedIn
- Email links to your training videos or past events and post the links on your website, blog, and social sites
- Send LinkedIn messages to each of your current contacts inviting them to attend your event
- You can also print up and mail or hand out tickets to your next event, so people have something physical in hand which increases the perceived value of the event.
- The key is to spread the word far and wide with people who are most likely to attend and invite others.

2. Develop Promotional Partnerships

Another great strategy that helps leverage the recommendations of others is to partner with businesses, charities, and associations that already serve your ideal patients. By offering to teach a class or give guest passes to your workshop as a gift to their clients, customers, members, and social media followers, you give them a high-perceived value item they can provide at no or low cost. The more you help them win patient loyalty, the more passionately they will promote your events and refer you to new patients.

We will cover this in detail in Chapter 16 on cross-promoting with your partners.

3. Invite Your Referral Partners to Invite Their Clients or Patients if Appropriate

There's no disputing the power of a personal recommendation. That's why one of the best ways to fill your seminars and workshops is to have your current and past referral practices attend your event. After all, as they share their personal story of the impact you had on their practice and patients, their patients will be much more inclined to schedule with your office and receive treatment from you.

4. Co-Produce Events with Others

One of the most effective ways to promote your event to a larger audience is to co-produce seminars or workshops with other specialists or supply sales representatives who are looking to attract the same ideal client profile. For example, suppose you are holding a Smile Makeover event and you invite all of your referring dental practices and prospective referring dental practices. In that case, you might consider partnering with your supply representative, who serves many general dental practices in the area.

By partnering and sharing the costs of promoting and producing your seminar or workshop, you help other businesses gain access to new prospects at a reduced marketing expense for everyone. Plus, as your partners get new patients from the event, they will promote you for other services they don't treat, since you are the reason that they won the business to begin with. This strategy also allows you to highly target your marketing while positioning you as the trusted expert and increasing your perceived credibility and expertise to a wider audience.

5. Speak at Other Events

There are numerous organizations that serve your ideal clients and are constantly looking for interesting speakers for their meetings and events. You gain tremendous credibility and visibility by volunteering to speak at events held by local businesses, Chambers of Commerce, banks, universities, the SBA, networking groups, and trade shows. Nonprofit organizations and associations that support and serve the healthcare market are also great opportunities to reach prospective patients. Any opportunity to speak in front of groups of people can lead you to more patients.

Once you have established your expertise throughout your training, the audience will be much more interested in attending your future workshops. Just be sure to include a closing slide that promotes your services and upcoming events. In addition, consider handing out worksheets that include details on your future workshops and offer your training services to those in need of a speaker. After all, sometimes, you need to do some shameless self-promotion to grow your business.

Be sure you have a call to action at the end of your presentation, letting your audience know the next steps you want them to take to move forward with you. Doing this each time you speak or teach will help fill your calendar with speaking engagements and bring more attendees to your events and clients to your business.

6. Offer Referral Rewards

Another great way to spread the word and expand your audience is to incentivize others to fill your events. You may be familiar with affiliate programs where businesses pay commissions on referrals that lead to sales, but have you ever considered offering to pay bounties or commissions to salespeople or marketing companies who help fill your events?

This strategy is especially effective when engaging marketing consultants or sales professionals who are used to working on a pay-for-performance basis. After all, these people speak with your target market every day and can easily promote your workshops and services.

Just be very specific about your perfect prospect profile, so they invite the right people who are most likely to do business with you. This strategy also works if you host online webinars as you can easily track attendees using a custom affiliate tracking code unique for each affiliate or promotional partner.

7. Outsource to Assistants or Interns

As a busy dentist, one of your biggest challenges is most likely time management. That's why you should consider delegating your promotional activities to an assistant or intern. This will help you maximize higher profit activities that you enjoy more. By training an assistant to manage your promotional activities, you focus your valuable time meeting with profitable prospects and clients.

Just use the list we've given you and create a plan for them to execute for you. If you don't already have staff who can help promote your events, just reach out to a local employment agency to hire a temp who can make the calls for you.

You can also contact a university or business school in your area and let them know you'd like to offer an internship for their students. You can usually find some great talent in the school of marketing with young adults eager to build their resumes and hungry for their first real job. While many will agree to do an unpaid internship with you, you may want to pay them a minimal hourly rate or a set amount for the quarter, so they are amply motivated. You can also make the internship unpaid but give them a bonus based on the number of attendees they help attract or actual clients that you close from the event.

These seven powerful strategies can help you fill your events with profitable prospects for your business. These strategies will also help you attract top, trusted pros which we will cover in the next chapter.

Scan this QR code or visit the link below for a video message about creating wealth through workshops:

https://ravingreferrals.com/workshops/

Chapter 12

Partner with Top Trusted Pros

When it comes to building a steady stream of Raving Referrals, one of the most underutilized and most effective strategies is to partner with other professionals who already serve your ideal patients. That's because businesses and professionals who are serving your perfect prospects consistently hear requests and opportunities for the services you provide. Plus, when a respected professional or business owner recommends you to their clients, customers, and contractors, it increases trust and accelerates revenue.

As Dr. Michael Hudson DDS of Hudson Dental and Orthodontics in Gilbert, AZ says,

> *"We get quite a few new patient referrals from Welch Physical Therapy. Their practice is located in our business complex, and they are a great referral partner for us. They are always sending people our way, so we refer people to them every chance we get."*

While a happy patient may know three or four ideal patients for you, a professional in a complementary industry may have three or four referrals for you each week or even each day. As you build your relationship and help them understand how you can help the people they serve, they will refer you a steady source of profitable prospects.

Your job is to help them see you and your service as the solution their clients and customers are looking for. Once they view you as a trusted solution helping them solve problems for their clients, they will refer you more often because you add value to both them and their customers.

> While many businesses focus most of their referral generation efforts on existing customers, the real untapped referral opportunity resides with strategic partners. In a recent survey I conducted on referrals, respondents felt that 30 percent of their referrals came from strategic partners. I think that should be more like 60 percent.
>
> **- John Jantsch**
> *The Referral Engine*

Over the past decade, we have surveyed thousands of business owners and professionals, asking them to identify how many referral partners they have who refer at least one new prospect every ninety days.

What has been surprising is that **32% of the professionals we surveyed said they had zero referral partners.** These people reported having to constantly scramble and hunt for new business because they had no one sending them profitable prospects. As a result, only half of the people in this group reported achieving an annual income of $50,000 or more.

The second group, which comprised **47% of total respondents, reported having one or two referral partners.** Although these people were getting a few referrals, they still found themselves in the bottom half of income earners in their companies or industries, with only 10% claiming to have achieved an annual income of $100,000 or more.

What was interesting was that the first two groups combined totaled 79% of everyone surveyed. Once again, the Pareto Principle (or 80/20 rule) proved to hold true.

The third group was made up of professionals who had three to nine referral partners, which equated to 19% of everyone surveyed. Over 70% of these people reported earning $100,000 or more per year, while under 20% of the first two groups achieved that income level.

Finally, the fourth group consisted of professionals claiming to have ten or more referral partners. What was shocking to our team was that only 2% of everyone who completed our survey was in this top group. Not surprisingly, this group reported much higher incomes, with all respondents claiming annual earnings over $100,000 and over half claiming annual income of more than $200,000 per year.

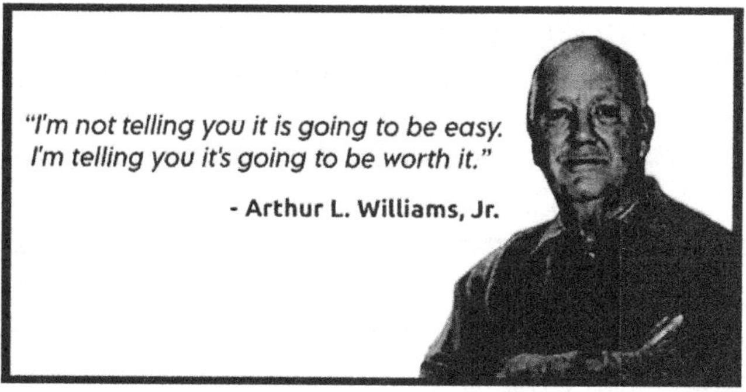

The Key to Success

I learned this strategy firsthand back in 1997 after starting as a mortgage loan officer. As I interviewed top producers in my firm and industry, I asked about their greatest source of business, and a common theme emerged.

All of the top producers I interviewed revealed that the bulk of their business came from a handful of professionals they had built referral partnerships with.

This is also true in dentistry. Although advertising can play an important role, social media is also an extension of the referral process. Depending on your community involvement, associations, friends, family, and general circle of influence, you will find that referrals are the key to your success.

According to Dr. Jed Huss, DDS, Diplomate with the International Congress of Oral Implantologists and owner of Restored Smiles Ranch:

> *"Surrounding yourself with great people and impactful partners will greatly accelerate the growth and success within your business. This principle rings true for myself and my Restored Smiles dental education company which has allowed me to have a greater impact within the field of dentistry and the lives of the doctors I teach.*
>
> *The success of your business is what you make of it. The more intentional and strategic your supporters and business partners are, the greater the impact you will be able to have."*

Assemble Your Power Team

To create your Power Team of trusted professionals committed to doing business with you, start by identifying the top industries that already serve your ideal clients.

In addition to The Champions Institute and ChampionDentists.com, I also run HOA.com, where we serve homeowners and are building the ***#1 Referral Network for Professionals Who Serve Homeowners***. Our company is literally in the business of helping people build their own trusted network of vetted and certified professionals who also serve homeowners. By helping these professionals connect, collaborate, and cross-promote each other, we help them generate more business by helping the people we serve together.

- Accountants
- Attorneys
- Bankers
- Business Coaches
- Carpet Cleaners
- Charities
- Chiropractors
- Cleaning Companies
- Credit Repair Experts
- Dentists
- Doctors
- Electricians
- Financial Advisors
- Garage Door Repair
- General Contractors
- Hair & Nail Salons
- Handymen
- Heating & AC Experts
- Insurance Agents
- Interior Designers
- Landscapers
- Locksmiths
- Marketing Consultants
- Massage Therapists
- Mobile IV Therapy
- Mortgage Pros
- Moving Companies
- New Home Builders
- Painters
- Personal Trainers
- Physical Therapists
- Photographers
- Pool Maintenance
- Plumbers
- Property Managers
- Real Estate Brokers
- Remodelers
- Restaurants
- Roofers
- Veterinarians
- Videographers
- Window & Door Experts

Consider the types of professionals you could consider building strategic alliances with. Look at people you tend to attract in your practice. Are there many people who seem to work within specific industries? Also consider looking at the community where your practice is located. Are there specific groups you can associate with? Specific companies that are located nearby? Are there any specific events that commonly or traditionally happen in your town that you can align with?

While you might receive patients from reps who work for select dental companies such as an implant company, you might also receive Raving Referrals from a parent group at particular schools. You might also find that by collaborating with local businesses, you all share non-competitive referrals.

Envision your community with your Perfect Patient in the center of the hub surrounded by all of the other possible referral collaborations.

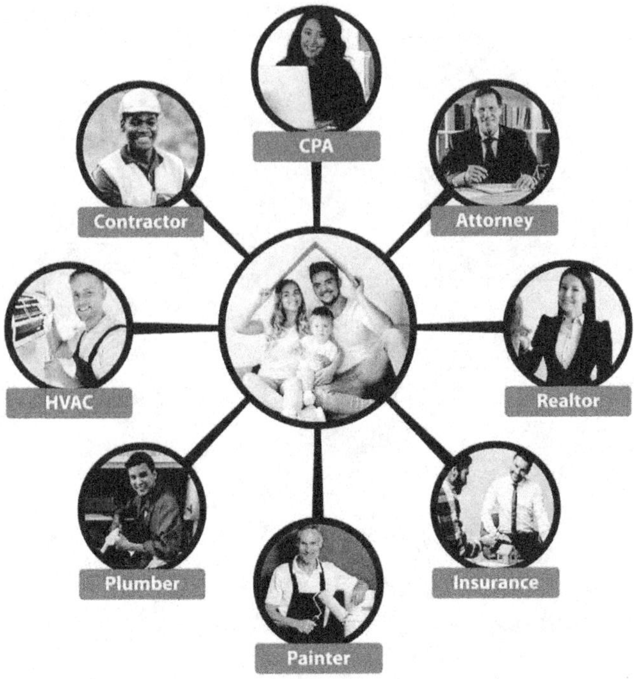

As you build your trusted team of referral partners, everyone will win more business together

So, the question is, who do you want on your trusted team?

> *"Creating referral partnerships with orthodontists and other dental specialists is incredibly beneficial for everyone involved. Not only does it help you provide superior service to your patients you also attract new patients to your practice from specialists who see patients every day but don't provide general dentistry."*
>
> *Dr. Jason Lipscomb D.D.S.*
> *Brush Up Dental & Shockoe Dentistry*

Identify Your Ideal Partners

What industries, local businesses, and specific service professionals do you want to build referral partnerships with? Review the proceeding list and write down key potential referral partners that can bring you the most business.

1. ______________________	11. ______________________
2. ______________________	12. ______________________
3. ______________________	13. ______________________
4. ______________________	14. ______________________
5. ______________________	15. ______________________
6. ______________________	16. ______________________
7. ______________________	17. ______________________
8. ______________________	18. ______________________
9. ______________________	19. ______________________
10. ______________________	20. ______________________

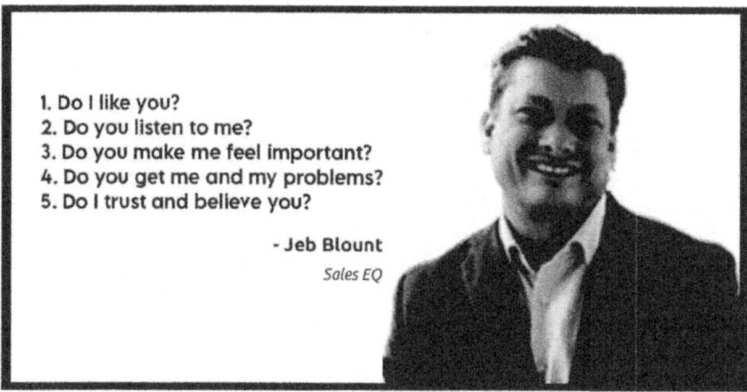

Prospective Partners

Most likely, you know several people in these professions you just listed. Perhaps you've known them for years or even decades and have never bothered to ask about doing business together. You may have family, friends, or other connections you've never pursued professionally. If that's true for you, I'm happy to tell you that you are sitting on an absolute goldmine.

What if you show them a win–win–win system where everyone prospers by working together?

As you help them understand who and how you help, many will gladly offer to promote you, especially when you approach professionals strategically, which we will cover shortly.

For each of the industries you've identified, start by asking yourself…

- Who do I already know, like, and trust in that industry?
- Who do I already refer business to?
- Who in each industry already refers business to me?

Asking these three questions will help you create a targeted list of complementary professionals who already know, like, and trust you. Since trust accelerates relationships, starting with people you know will dramatically speed up your referrals and revenue.

The truth is that you serve these professionals every day in your practice. But have you ever taken the time to learn who your patients are and what they do professionally. Many of the people sitting in your operatories are influencers in business and many have a large social sphere.

That's why we recommend you consider partnering with your patients and letting them know you would like to help promote them and their business to the patients and community you serve. Imagine if you had 20, 50 or even 100 passionate promoters for your practice.

Think about Realtors® or mortgage brokers for example. These people are helping new homeowners move into your community every day. Wouldn't you love them to recommend your practice to every new family that moves into the neighborhoods surrounding your practice? By simply promoting them on your website, social media or through a brochure or community bulletin board in your office, you add value to them and their business.

We will cover co-marketing campaigns in chapter 16, but for now, start thinking about the people you serve and how you might partner with them and grow your businesses together.

The Proven Referral Partner Script:

Once you've identified your prospective partners, it's time to approach these professionals strategically. If you are not comfortable making these calls, consider hiring or promoting someone to your team who can serve as your Community Ambassador doing business development on behalf of your practice.

After twenty-plus years of testing, here's what we've found works best for creating profitable partnerships. If you follow this proven script below, you'll have people lining up to meet with you.

Just say…

> *"Hi (name), the reason I'm calling is that I'm creating a team of professionals I'll be recommending to all my patients. I was thinking about you because I have a lot of patients who could benefit from your services. I'd love to sit down with you to discuss the possibility of adding you to my team and promoting you. When's a good time to get together and strategize?"*

Imagine receiving that call from someone you've known for years who serves your ideal patients all day long. Wouldn't you be excited about the possibility of having them consistently referring clients to you? Of course, you would! As long as they are someone you know, like, and trust.

When you follow this proven process, you can quickly create new referral partnerships with ease.

But how do you create partnerships with target professions when you don't know anyone in that field?

Great question. Glad you asked.

Filling Gaps

As you start creating strategic alliances and profitable partnerships, there will undoubtedly be some gaps. You may find a few industries or professions where you don't know anyone in that field. That's when asking patients to introduce you to top professionals they know, like, and trust is a powerful way to expand your team and your referral business.

Asking your VIP patients to introduce you to their top professional service providers gives you quick and easy access to high-quality professionals with whom it otherwise might be challenging to develop a relationship.

The good news is that asking patients for introductions is extremely easy when you know how. It also quickens your velocity to create profitable partnerships.

First, identify the profession to which you want to be introduced. Let's say you want to get connected with a quality CPA, for example. Just call up your client, or while sitting with them, simply say:

> *"Thanks so much for your time today. I'd like to ask for your help. As you may know, I am in the process of expanding my practice, and I'm looking for a great CPA I can refer my patients to. I'm wondering if you know of any good CPAs you think I should meet. I'm planning to meet and interview two or three, and your CPA will be one of those I would like to meet with, not just for my personal business but also for the opportunity to refer patients to them. Is there anyone you'd recommend I meet with?"*

Once you ask, shut up and let them talk. It's normal to want to fill the space if they don't speak immediately but hold back and give them a few moments to think about who they can introduce you to. You will find most patients will be happy to help and introduce you to other professionals they use. Plus, since the introduction is coming from a mutual client, you already have something in common to start building rapport and trust with the other pro.

You can also post your request on social media. Not only will you increase the number of introductions you receive, but you will also let your patients and social sphere know they can turn to you and your team whenever they need help. You will be amazed to see top, trusted professionals reaching out to you proactively.

This strategy works extremely well because people love to help others. By giving them an opportunity to make an introduction, they are helping both you and the other professional they are introducing.

Ask for an Intro

Once your contact recommends someone for you to connect with, it's best to set the stage for the conversation. Just ask your contact to make an introduction and share the person's phone number so you can follow up proactively.

Simply say,

> *"Thanks so much for the introduction. Would you be willing to make a quick call or send them a text to tell them how we know each other and that I will be calling them (date and time of scheduled call)?*
>
> *Is there anything you think I should know before I call them?"*

WIN–WIN–WIN

Using this approach, the person to whom you are being introduced will be expecting and even looking forward to your call... all before you even dial their digits.

Once you've been introduced, simply call the professional at the appointed time, mention your client's name, and share that they come highly recommended by your mutual client. This creates instant connection and is the common ground that opens the door and fast-tracks a mutually prosperous partnership.

By reaching out to professionals you already know, like, and trust – and then filling the gaps with quality introductions from key clients and colleagues – you can quickly gain access to great professionals and build a powerfully profitable referral team.

Put the power of partnerships to work for your business.

Scan this QR code or visit the link below for a video message about partnering with top trusted pros who serve your perfect prospects every day:

https://ravingreferrals.com/partner/

Chapter 13

Network Strategically

Another way to meet prospective referral partners is by attending networking events or study clubs. In every city, there are dozens of monthly opportunities to meet other professionals. Typically hosted and led by local chambers of commerce, local dentists or specialists or professional networking companies, these groups exist to help professionals and business owners connect and collaborate. That means everyone in attendance is there for the same reason you are – to meet new people in hopes of doing business together.

Have a Plan

Before investing any time going to a networking event, be sure you have a plan for who, where, and how.

- Who do you want to meet?
- Where do they usually meet?
- How will you meet them?

First, get crystal clear on the type of people you want to meet.

Second, find out where these people connect and congregate. Research local groups or events where your ideal referral partners meet and get together.

The best way to do this is to call your top referral partners and ask what groups they belong to or recommend. If they belong to a chamber of commerce or networking group, you'll find them eager to invite you as their guest. These organizations typically track how many guests each member introduces to the group, so inviting guests is encouraged and celebrated.

Third, have a plan for how you will meet your ideal connections. There may only be one or two great contacts for you in the room. Rather than walking around randomly introducing yourself to strangers, ask the people running the event to introduce you to the people you want to meet.

Since the event leaders check everyone in as they arrive, they meet each and every person who walks through the door. That means they are perfectly positioned to help you. You just need to ask for your ideal introduction, which is super easy when you use the following script.

Once you've checked in to the event, simply smile and say,

> *"I'm wondering if you can help me. The primary reason I'm here is to find a top (CPA) that I can refer clients to and build a referral partnership with. Can you tell me if there are any quality (CPA)'s here I can connect with?"*

The beauty of this question is that you are actually helping them be successful in their job. After all, the reason they are at the event is to help members and attendees connect, collaborate, and cross-refer each other. By asking for an introduction to the precise professionals you are looking to connect with, you make it easy for them to help you.

Top 10 Tips for Networking Strategically

After attending and leading networking events from coast to coast, I've learned there are ten top tips for networking success:

1. Visualize Success – Success starts long before you walk into any meeting or event. Remember, just one referral partner can double your business in a year or even less. As you think about the event, visualize exactly who you want to meet. Get clear on the industry they are in and have a plan for how you would like to work together. Then, before the event, take a few moments and envision yourself having a great time meeting an incredible referral partner in that industry who has been looking for someone just like you to help their clients. As you visualize the future you want to create, you activate the law of attraction, which is always good to have working for you.
2. Bring A Buddy – Invite one of your referral partners to join you and work the room together. Before the event, get clear on who each person is looking to meet. Then, as you meet a potential match for your referral partner, make an enthusiastic introduction to the person you just met. This helps you add value to both parties and elevate your status in their eyes. Be sure to praise and edify your networking buddy to help them feel good and raise their perceived status. As you help your referral partners succeed, they will naturally return the favor and go out of their way to help you in return. WIN–WIN–WIN.
3. Meet The Leaders – Introduce yourself to the people hosting the event. They are often servant leaders dedicated to helping people succeed. Since they have the respect of the members, when they make an introduction, people take the meeting. Befriend these folks, and you will win faster.
4. Ask For Introductions – Ask the event leaders for introductions to the top pros they know in your target profession. Simply say,

"The main reason I am here is that I'm looking for a quality (CPA) to whom I can refer my clients. Do you happen to know any good (CPA)s you would recommend I connect with?"

If they know trustworthy people in that industry, they will be happy to help and make an introduction.

5. Be Confident – First impressions matter. As you meet new people, smile, look them in the eye, and introduce yourself confidently with a firm handshake. When you exude confidence, people feel it. Especially if they have a high nurturing personality style. The truth is that while you are interviewing potential partners, they are evaluating you as well. Show them you are comfortable in your own skin and confident in your ability to get the job done right. Your confidence will give them confidence in you.
6. Ask Quality Questions – Show you are interested by asking great questions to learn about the people you're meeting. If you aren't a natural networker, just ask:
   - Who? What? When? Where? Why?
   - Who is your ideal client?
   - What is the primary problem you solve?
   - When do people most need your services?
   - Where do you get most of your clients currently?
   - Why did you choose this industry?

The answers to these questions will give you quick clarity as to how well you trust this person and how well they match your perfect partner profile.

7. Listen And Learn – You're here to meet good people to partner with, not to sell. After asking each question, really listen to what the person is telling you. Study what they say both verbally and non-verbally. You'll learn a lot about

them in a very short time. As you listen, ask yourself if you like this person and can see yourself eventually feeling comfortable referring your clients to them.

8. Schedule A Discovery Call – Your primary goal for attending any networking event should be to schedule one-on-one discovery calls with Perfect Prospects or referral partners. Rather than trying to have a meaningful conversation in a busy, crowded, noisy environment, ask to schedule a one-on-one call at a later date. When you find someone who may be a fit, simply say,

   "From what you've shared, I have a number of contacts who might benefit from what you do. Can we get together another time so I can ask you a few questions? Maybe next Tuesday afternoon or Wednesday morning?

   What works best for you?"

9. Be Brief, Be Brilliant, Be Gone – Once you have synced calendars and scheduled a discovery call, thank them for their time and excuse yourself from the conversation. Don't overstay your welcome. Always leave them wanting more.
10. Follow-Up and Follow-Through – As you know, the fortune is in the follow-up. After the event, think about each person you met and send an email, text, or direct message to those with whom you want to explore relationships. If you scheduled a discovery call, send a calendar invite with the date, time, and location or description of how you will connect. You may also want to send a friend or connection request on social media to accelerate the trust-building process.

When you follow these top ten networking tips, you will build your referral team quickly and easily.

Networking Groups

In addition to referral mixers and events, you may also want to join a chamber of commerce, MeetUp, or a structured referral group like LeTip and BNI. While chambers allow unlimited members per industry, referral groups often only allow one member per profession, which is great if they have an opening in your industry.

When I was starting out in the mortgage business, I joined a chapter of LeTip International in Beaverton, Oregon. The fifteen members of this chapter met for breakfast every Thursday at 7:00 am sharp. Breaking bread together each week was a great way to get to know each other and build long-term relationships and referral partnerships. It was awesome to have a team of people committed to helping each other win and constantly scouting for opportunities for each other.

In 2013, I was referred to LeTip CEO Kim Marie Branch-Pettid, a wonderful woman committed to helping businesses grow faster together. Having visited her international headquarters many times and spent time with her, her husband, and her executive teams over the years, I can tell you her organization goes above and beyond to help their members grow their businesses, with chapters nationwide from coast-to-coast. Each chapter hosts a weekly online or in-person meeting, along with evening mixer events and large-scale conferences.

The entire LeTip referral machine has been built to ensure every member receives massive value. Each chapter has officers who lead the meetings following a regimented agenda set by LeTip headquarters. Guests are welcomed warmly and thrilled to find so many opportunities to build relationships with quality professionals.

After announcements are made, each attendee is asked to quickly stand and share their message of who and how they help. Then they report new referrals and business opportunities they have given or received from members of the group.

Referrals are tracked on their proprietary Wired platform which helps each club track and measure the business passed and the return on investment (ROI) each member has received from the group. Those who refer most are celebrated and sought after. To search for a LeTip chapter in your area, visit LeTip.com.

Dr. Ivan Misner took the LeTip concept and created his own organization called Business Networking International (BNI) back in January of 1985. Over the decades, this organization has grown to be a global powerhouse with over 270,000 members worldwide.

Although I've never been an official BNI member, I've attended countless chapter meetings and conferences over the decades. I've also had the great honor and pleasure of meeting BNI founder Dr. Ivan Misner, who is largely considered the godfather of networking. He is a humble servant eager to educate and empower as many people as possible. That's just one of the reasons BNI members are so passionate and loyal to the BNI company and community. With over 9,500 chapters, you can find a group near you at BNI. com.

The largest event-based networking organization in the U.S. is Network After Work. Rather than weekly alliance meetings, they host monthly mixer events in every major market in the U.S. Network After Work has hosted over 4,000 events over the past decade attracting over 600,000 attendees. Over that time, they have created over fifteen million business connections, which is an astonishing accomplishment.

Every Network After Work event I've attended has had over 100 guests and had plenty of prominent people to connect with. One of their brilliant networking innovations is using color coded name badges to instantly convey the industry you are in. That helps you work quickly to identify people in the industries in which you are looking to connect.

Network After Work now offers virtual events and online education as well to complement the in-person events they produce. What impresses me most about their events is that they attract the highest quality people I've met at any networking event I've ever been to.

While most networking groups tend to attract small business owners and professionals, Network After Work events also attract executives and decision makers from major corporations. This is much more of a white-collar crowd, so it's an excellent gathering place if you're looking to meet B2B clients or referral partners.

Check out their schedule of events at NetworkAfterWork.com.

We've compiled a list of great networking organizations and referral groups at the end of this book. There's no substitute for meeting people in the real world, so go find a local group and start networking strategically.

THE FORTUNE IS IN THE FOLLOW-UP

As you start networking, you will be meeting some awesome people that can send you a lot of business. Your goal should be to get into the know, like, trust zone as quickly as possible.

Connect with them on social media and be sure to like, comment, share, retweet, and invite them often and you can accelerate the trust building process.

A tactic I learned from Casey Eberhart in his awesome Networking Riches course is his ATM social strategy:

1. ADD people to your FB group
2. TAG them in the post
3. MESSAGE them personally

Do this consistently and you'll start attracting great referral partners who send you a steady stream of Perfect Prospects.

Before you attend another networking event,
be sure to scan this QR code or visit the link below
to learn the top three networking quick tips.

Share with your professional network to add value
and help them accelerate their success:

https://Ravingreferrals.com/network

Chapter 14

Create Your Referral Alliance

As you start cross-promoting and cross-referring with other business owners and professionals, over time you will build strong trusted relationships that generate a lot of new patients for your practice. The key is to find people you enjoy spending time with and then intentionally spend more time with them. Creating a formal Referral Alliance will help you accelerate this process so referrals flow faster.

Connect With Connectors

After working for many years in industries unrelated to dentistry, one day, Julieanne became close friends with a dentist who had an office across the street from her home. She intentionally built friendships that led to referral partnerships.

As she explains, *"In addition to our close proximity, we both had a mutual love of art. My husband and I opened an art gallery in the same town. My dentist friend also had a gallery inside his practice where he hosted gatherings regularly for the community. Both of our families began supporting the local art scene while growing our mutual trust and respect for one another. This soon led beyond art, and he introduced me to an entirely new friend group and network of hard-working dental professionals. I understood that by building friendships with each individual dentist, I was able to connect with this entire network of dental professionals. These people had built deep trust with each other and the more relational equity I built with each member of the friend group, the more I was welcomed into their collective circle of trust.*

My business of social media was no different and I was very successful at serving dentists. However, I had seen too many practice owners be burned by people who were out to make a quick buck. I knew I wanted to work with quality dentists so I delivered value knowing that my commitment to delivering massive value would earn their trust and referrals over time. I understood that trust takes time to build, especially with those who may have had poor experiences in the past. I knew the best way to grow my business was to deliver real results and leverage the relationships and reputation I'd built within this trusted circle of friends and associates. The more value I delivered, the more they trusted me and introduced me to others within the community."

Connecting with connectors through people who already know, like and trust you can make a significant impact on your business. In addition, by helping others with their businesses you can take collaboration to a mutually beneficial place where everyone benefits and has an incentive to work together.

Invite Your Trusted Team

If you are serious about taking your business to new heights, consider starting your own personal referral group or what we call a Referral Alliance. For best results, bring together your best referral partners and ask them to join you in launching your own group. As you unite your team, you elevate your status and establish yourself as a leader and influential connector.

The best way to accomplish this quickly and easily is to schedule a meeting at your office, a restaurant, or even via zoom. Simply choose a time and location then send a quick message to each person inviting them to attend.

Say something like:

> "Hi (name), as you may know, I am in the process of expanding my practice, and I'm creating an alliance of vetted and trusted professionals I can refer my patients to. I truly value our relationship and would like to invite you to be a core member of my referral team. I will be gathering my most important referral partners (date/time) at (location) and hope you can attend.
>
> Please let me know if you can join us."

I recommend you consider outsourcing the coordination of a calendar invite to each person you want to attend so they have the date, time, and location already in their calendar. That makes it super easy for them to accept your invite with one quick click. This also helps you see who is interested, available, and committed to attending. You may also want to create an event on Facebook, LinkedIn, or another social network if you are connected to these people on those platforms.

Your Alliance Meeting

As your group gathers, you may have a few early arrivals. Welcome them warmly and let them know when your meeting will begin. If you are not an extrovert or natural nurturer, you may want to have an assistant greet your guests, so they feel the love from the get-go.

Start your meeting by greeting the group and thanking them for attending. Ask each person to introduce themselves and describe who they help and how they help. Once everyone has introduced themselves, simply review some of the co-marketing campaigns outlined in the *Referral Partner Blueprint* outlined in Chapter 16.

Here's a script you can use as a guideline:

Greeting:

> "Thank you for coming today. The reason I asked you all to join me is that I am expanding my practice and creating an alliance of vetted and trusted professionals I'll be referring my patients to.
>
> I truly value each and every one of you and view you as one of the best in your respective industries. Not only am I hoping to do more business with you personally, but I also want to connect each of you so you can do more business together.
>
> After all, everyone in this room serves (consumers, homeowners, businessowners, parents, professionals, etc.), so we share the same ideal client and can grow our businesses faster and further by cross-referring and cross-promoting each other."

Introductions

> What I'd like to do now is go around the room and give everyone a chance to introduce themselves and share who you help and how you help. That will help everyone here understand the services you provide and who your perfect prospects and ideal clients are.
>
> Before you leave, I'd like to ask you each to fill out a Referral Partner Optimization Form so I can train my team on what type of patients we should refer to you.
>
> I'll go first. As you all know, my name is and I help ____________ (share your Service Statement).
>
> To give you an example of what I do, I recently had a client who ____________________________. (share

a story of a problem you solved and the difference it made for them).

I'm passionate about helping people __________ and a great referral for me is a (share your Perfect Prospect Profile). Before we move on, does anyone have any questions about my expertise or what specific services I provide?

Answer any questions that come up and remember to tell success stories so people can visualize who and how you help. Telling a memorable story of someone you've helped turns people into referral scouts because when they hear someone facing the challenge you solve, they will immediately think of you.

"Hopefully, that gives you more clarity on how I can help your clients and customers. Now let's go around the room starting to my left."

After each person shares who and how they help, be sure to compliment and edify them to boost their confidence and status among your guests. Your job is to help everyone feel honored and special.

Share stories of how these people have helped you or your patients in the past. Describe what you appreciate most about each person, and you will instantly expand your value in their eyes. This process ensures people view you as the connector and influencer you are. It also locks in their loyalty and commitment to doing business with you going forward.

Instructions

Once all attendees have shared who and how they help, share your plan for doing more business together. Using the *Referral Partner Blueprint* in Chapter 16 as a guide, mention some of the strategies you plan to use to introduce your trusted referral partners to your clients and colleagues. This will give them a vision for how they will win more business through your Referral Alliance.

We recommend your strategy include interviews with your referral partners to add value to them and build their credibility in the eyes of your clients. Simply record a quick zoom interview and post the video recording on Facebook, YouTube, and/or LinkedIn. Alternatively, you can broadcast your conversation live on these platforms as well.

Wrap-Up

As you conclude your Alliance meeting, thank each person for attending and let them know you'd like to schedule a one-to- one conversation with them to plan out how you can grow your businesses together. Be sure each person leaves with your Referral Kit, business cards, referral cards, brochures, and any other marketing materials you'd like them to give to their clients when they recommend your services. That way, each Referral Partner leaves empowered to refer you quickly and consistently.

Hang-Out

If your schedule allows, recommend they hang out and connect with the people in the room who would be the best fit for their business. You will add additional value by connecting them with other business owners and professionals with whom they can build relationships. Plus, the more time you spend with each person, the more likely they are to send profitable prospects your way.

Consider printing a form each Partner fills out so you have a written record of who they help, how they help, how they want to be referred, and a success story you can share with your clients.

Raving Referrals Partner Profile

Name: ______________________________

Company: ______________________________

Profession: ______________________________

Phone: ______________________________

Who are your Perfect Prospects?

How would you describe your perfect prospects and ideal clients?

____

____

____

How do you help?

What is most important for me to share about your product or service? What makes you unique?

____

____

____

How would you like me to refer you?

Do you offer free consultations or any special promotions you'd like me to share?

____

____

____

What's your best success story?

Share your best client result or testimonial so I can retell the story to my clients.

____

____

____

Following these steps will help you create a highly productive and profitable referral alliance you can build your business with for years to come. The best part is that a client for one of you can be a client for all of you. Once you attract a new client for your business, think about which of your referral partners you can introduce them to. There are likely other services this client would benefit from. As you refer them to your partners, and they refer their clients to you, everyone wins together.

Building a strong Referral Alliance can help you attract Raving Referrals for years to come.

Scan this QR code or visit the link below for a
video message about creating powerful and profitable
partnering with companies and professionals
who are committed to your success:

https://ravingreferrals.com/alliance

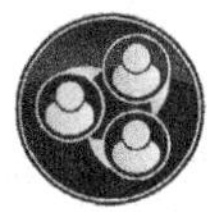

Chapter 15

The Referral Partner Blueprint

The fastest and easiest way to build referral partnerships is by using the *Referral Partner Blueprint.* This easy-to-use system gives you a paint-by-numbers approach to guide people through a collaboration conversation.

Once you've identified someone you would like to form a referral partnership with, simply pull out the *Referral Partner Blueprint* to guide your conversation.

Discuss the cross-promotion strategies you think will work best for this particular referral partnership. Check off what each person is willing to do for the other so both parties have a clear agreement in place.

As you follow the format and fill in the blanks, you will find it makes the process of creating referral partnerships with complementary professionals simple.

Referral Partner Blueprint

To create a mutually prosperous relationship, both parties agree to

- Introduce each other to prospective referral partners
- Recommend each other to clients & colleagues
- Invite each other to participate in joint client consultations if appropriate
- Cross-Promote each other through:

01. Introductions
02. Client Referrals
03. Rating and Reviews
04. Special Offers
05. Gift Certificates
06. Consultations
07. Referral Cards
08. Websites
09. Social Posts
10. Newsletters
11. Team Brochures
12. Bundled Offers
13. Direct Mail
14. Client Events
15. Sponsorships
16. Workshops
17. Podcasts
18. Video Interviews
19. Webinars
20. Referral Mixers
21. Charity Champions Campaigns

We will cover each of these cross-promotion campaigns in the next chapter. First, you need to understand how to educate and empower your referral partners to send you new patient opportunities quickly and consistently.

Train Your Team

As you start using the *Referral Partner Blueprint*, you will find people are eager to partner with you. That's why it's important to train your referral partners on the specific clients you are looking for, and how best to refer you.

To ensure you attract a steady stream of profitable prospects coming to your business, follow these five proven steps:

1. Discuss your *Perfect Prospect Profile* and *Service Statement* so they understand how you help and what challenges you solve.
2. Share stories of patients you've helped so they will remember and refer you when a client mentions facing a similar challenge.
3. Supply them with your Referral Kit including brochures and business cards they can set out in their lobby and give to their clients.
4. Create customized gift certificates or referral cards so your referral partner feels special, and their clients know you are a trusted professional.
5. Print a list of your top ten Frequently Asked Questions (FAQs) so your referral partners are informed and can educate their clients about the services you provide.

These are the top five ways you can empower your partners. The key is to help them understand what sets you apart so you become their go-to, number one trusted resource for each and every client of theirs who is looking for a great dentist or specialist like you. The more you educate your referral partners on the value you provide, the more potential patients they will send your way. So long as you follow up consistently.

Follow-Up and Follow Through

After you've met with each prospective referral partner, be sure to follow up and follow through on any commitments you made.

Take action immediately, and you will impress them with your professionalism. If you have committed to making introductions, make them quickly and effectively. Go above and beyond to gain your new referral partners respect and reciprocity.

Be sure to update and thank the person who made the introduction. Give them an overview of how well the conversation went and whether you believe this person will be a fit for your clients. Following up honors the introducer and shows them you take good care of the introductions they give you. Often, this alone leads to more referrals because you are demonstrating your professionalism in communication.

If you're really serious about building a solid referral base, you may want to send whoever introduced you a thank you card or small gift as a token of appreciation. This will lead them one step closer to singing your praises to everyone they know. The more people feel you care, the more they will care about you.

Play the Long Game

One thing you need to understand is that building referral partnerships takes time. Although you will likely receive referrals from some partners quickly, others will need to know, like and trust you over time. The more relational equity you build with people, the more referrals you will receive.

Rather than expecting instant results, make a goal for how many referral partnerships you plan to create over the coming year. Keeping your eye on the prize will help you build a solid business that will generate profitable prospects for years to come.

Connect with the people you want to do business with regularly. Calendar consistent communications to them every two weeks at a minimum. Seeing them in person always creates the deepest connections but isn't the most time efficient. That's why you want to mix in regular phone calls, text messages, video messages, emails, and social media messages to stay top-of-mind and continually add value.

Before reaching out, think of a way you can add value to them and their clients. Never call saying you are just "checking in". That is one of the worst statements you can make because you are telling them you have no other reason to call other than to ask them for business. Instead, you could:

- Give them a referral.
- Provide an update on a client they referred.
- Offer to connect them with a professional or business owner.
- Share an idea you think will help their business.
- Ask a question about their industry or the services they provide.
- Offer to promote them using one of the co-marketing
- campaigns in the next chapter.
- Invite them to join you at an industry or networking event.
- Let them know about new offers or services you are adding.
- Share industry insights you think they should know about.
- Stop by to drop off gifts, books, brochures, or branded swag.

It's A Numbers Game

Using these strategies and scripts can make a profound impact on your business over the months and years to come. Just imagine what your business will look like 12 months from now if you take the time to meet just one new prospective partner each week for the next year.

Of those 50 people, if only 20% are a fit and become your referral partners, you will have 10 new professionals referring you profitable patients consistently for years to come. Then, for the rest of your career, you will be on easy street never having to wonder where your next patient is coming from. In reality, most professionals experience much better results than partnering 20% of the time, so you can truly accelerate the process and your revenue by following the *Referral Partner Blueprint*.

Give More

When building referral partnerships, you should always be on the lookout for ways to add value to your partners. Truth is that the more you give in life, the more will be given to you. I'm such a passionate proponent of this strategy that I had customized license plates for my BMW back in Oregon that said, GIV MOR.

For me, it's much more than just a slogan. It's a life philosophy. I'm always looking to add value to everyone I meet and to give as much as humanly possible. When you adopt the GIVE MORE attitude and look for ways to practice random acts of kindness, you'll find life becomes easier in ways you would never have imagined. This might sound a little woo-woo to you right now, but in my experience, karma and the law of attraction are very real. The more you give, the more serendipity shows up in your life.

Back in 1998, my wife and I took a two-week trip to Italy and Greece. While it was tough to leave my mortgage business for two weeks, I made sure to bring back some exotic gifts for the Realtors with whom I was building referral partnerships. In addition to some of the standard tourist trinkets, I also brought back metal bottles filled with Greek Ouzo, as well as the most delicious baklava I have ever tasted.

When I returned home and dropped off these sweet treats and exotic liqueurs to my top referral partners, they were blown away that I was thoughtful enough to think of them while on my European vacation. Especially since I had transported these gifts over 6,000 miles to bring them back something special.

Next, I traveled to Hawaii and brought back cases of chocolate covered macadamia nuts. While my referral partners enjoyed the gift, what they really appreciated is that they were important enough to me that I was thinking of them while away with my family.

The truth is that those tasty treats helped solidify relationships and win referrals worth thousands of times the cost of the gifts. While I'm sure they enjoyed what I gave them, what won them over was my generosity and thoughtfulness.

Often in dentistry, you will see that reps from dental supply companies are taken for granted by dentists and their teams. It is often overlooked that they themselves may reside in your practice's neighborhood or may be connected to associations you hadn't even considered as potential referral partners.

The opportunity to pull in dental supply company reps as part of your family is one that is undeniably neglected in dentistry. Imagine if instead of looking at a rep as a salesperson, you began to consider how you might further help them with their business. What if you treated them like VIP partners only to figure out new ways you might be able to collaborate beyond a simple purchase from them?

As you start building your referral partnerships, be on the lookout for ways you can make a difference in their lives. Do everything you can to give more to your partners, and you will activate the law of reciprocity and watch your business grow.

Especially when you start cross-promoting with your partners, which is the final key to profitable partnerships.

Ready to create more profitable partnerships?

The *Referral Partner Blueprint* makes it easy to guide your conversations and create a powerful plan where you and your referral partners get into action and win together

Scan this QR code or visit the link below for a video message on how to use the *Referral Partner Blueprint* to maximize your success:

https://ravingreferrals.com/blueprint

Chapter 16

Top 21 Cross Promotion Campaigns

Marketing is the lifeblood of your business. Marketing is what spreads the message that brings in profitable prospects that become lifetime clients. That's why partnering and cross promoting with others who already serve your market can be the fastest and most powerful way to grow your business.

When it comes to promoting yourself and your services, there's nothing like the credibility and visibility you gain when someone else raves about you. People don't care what you say about yourself near as much as they care what others say about you.

Your goal is to get seen, get found, and get paid.

When people see your name or brand being recommended by someone they respect, they automatically trust you more and are more likely to consider you. Especially when people endorse you authentically and passionately.

Whether your goal is to attract a few ideal patients, or gain millions of fans and followers, cross promoting with influencers, experts, businesses, and professionals who serve your ideal clients can produce real results rapidly.

You've Seen This Before

Often called co-op marketing or simply co-marketing, this is a strategic marketing and advertising partnership between two or more companies or referral partners who promote each other to their respective audiences. Collaborating on a marketing campaign can help both parties generate twice the results with half the effort.

What's great about co-marketing is that both partners leverage their social sphere to generate more buzz, awareness, fans, followers, and profitable prospects together. These campaigns can quickly provide the extra boost that attracts more leads and revenues.

Even if you have never co-marketed yourself, you've seen the biggest brands on the planet doing it for years. One of the best examples is the shoe brand Nike partnering with Michael Jordan to create the Air Jordan brand. According to Forbes magazine, their partnership has generated over $1.3 billion to Michael Jordan since 1984. This alliance not only made Jordan richer than any contract from playing basketball, but it also simultaneously solidified Nike as the dominant leader in the shoe game. In Nike's 2019 fiscal year, the Jordan Brand generated $3.1 billion in sales accounting for 8% of total Nike revenue for the year.

Back in Portland, one of the fathers whose boys I coached in youth sports was the son of Reggie Saunders, Nike's Senior Director of Entertainment Marketing for Air Jordan. He was one cool cat. His stock really rose with the boys on our basketball team when he gave each player a free pair of the latest and greatest brand spanking new Air Jordans. Reggie told me story after story of the athletes the company was able to attract as partners because these players grew up wearing Air Jordans and always wanted to "Be like Mike."

The value Jordan brought Nike went far beyond shoe sales and solidified the brand as the king of the shoe game. As Nike would say, when it comes to co-marketing, JUST DO IT.

A holistic dental practice who is a client of mine recently began working on a campaign specifically to promote other holistic practitioners to their patients. They are creating a wall in their lobby dedicated to these referral partners. In addition, they will offer exclusive discounts on their dental services to the patients and customers of the companies they feature in their lobby. It's a win-win for everyone involved.

Here are a few co-marketing examples to get your wheels spinning:

CoverGirl Makeup & Star Wars

Another great example of creating profitable partnerships and co-marketing campaigns comes from the larger-than-life Shaquille O'Neal. After having a hall-of-fame career on the court, Shaq cashed in on his notoriety by creating strategic alliances with a number of companies and brands, including:

- 24-Hour Fitness
- AZ Beverage Company
- Auntie Anne's Pretzels
- Boys & Girls Club of America
- Buick
- Carnival Cruise
- Comcast
- Dove
- Dunkman Shoes
- Epsom Printers
- Five Guys Burgers & Fries
- Gold Bond
- Icy Hot
- JC Penney
- Krispy Kreme
- Lining Shoes
- Macy's
- Monster Headphones
- Muscle Milk
- NBA 2K
- Nestle Crunch
- Papa John's Pizza
- Pepsi
- Reebok
- Sleep Apnea Mask
- Soupman
- Susta Sugar Substitute
- Taco Bell
- The General Insurance
- Zales Jewelry

While you may never collaborate with a major corporation like those listed above, the strategy is the same when promoting your services.

Think about simple co-marketing campaigns you might be able to act on within your community. This could be as basic as promoting a next-door restaurant by using a gift card for dinner in one of your promotions. Or it could be more complex such as in co-branding for press releases and in advertising with anyone from a supplier to a toothpaste brand for example. If you market your own products as well, there are countless ideas to co-market products within dentistry as well.

Now that you are aware of co-marketing campaigns, you are going to start seeing these campaigns over and over. The power and influence you can unlock through partnerships are unmatched. In fact, teenagers are now making millions as instant influencers on Instagram and TikTok partnering with companies as brand ambassadors to promote their energy drinks, clothing, makeup, and jewelry products.

Within dentistry, you might look at what patients you currently have and see if there are opportunities to work with existing influencers within your practice. Earned media can generate a tremendous return for every dollar you invest in a collaboration of this nature. Consider the example of a dentist I worked with who agreed to offer clear aligners to an influencer who initially had a fast growing following but who wasn't yet famous at the point that I introduced them.

That particular influencer documented every appointment through video posts which led to archivable and reusable content of the journey of the patient with the practice. The doctor is now able to use all the content ongoing on his own site and his own social media. The influencer ended up going on to become one of the most famous kids in America.

The Ultimate Trust Transfer

Co-marketing gives you the ultimate marketing leverage because as you cross promote your referral partners, they transfer the trust they've built with their clients and prospects on to you.

By collaborating and cross promoting each other, both you and your partner:

- Increase awareness for each other's businesses and services
- Attract more prospects, fans, and followers
- Generate leads, referrals, and business opportunities
- Reduce marketing costs while increasing closing rates

Creating cross promotions and co-marketing campaigns with just ten other professionals or businesses over the next year can increase your marketing reach by 1,000% or more. The way this works is simple. Let's say your ideal patients are homeowners and that you have 1,000 people on your mailing list. If you partner with ten other professionals who also serve homeowners with similar size databases, you are now being promoted, endorsed, and recommended to 10,000 prospective clients in addition to your own 1,000 contacts.

Plus, by helping your partners gain more visibility and grow their books of business, you dramatically increase the likelihood they will return the favor by promoting and referring you to their patients and colleagues.

So how can you leverage the power of co-marketing to promote your practice in your local market?

Glad you asked!

21 Top Cross Promotion Campaigns

As you meet with prospective Referral Partners to create a strategic alliance, just pull out your *Referral Partner Blueprint* to guide your conversation. This powerful tool will help you steer your discussions through the various ways you and your partners can cross-promote each other to win more business together.

The basic strategy for each of these campaigns is for you and your partners to promote and recommend each other to your respective databases and social spheres.

The top 21 ways you and your partners can proactively promote or recommend each other are:

1. Introductions
2. Client Referrals
3. Ratings & Reviews
4. Special Offers
5. Gift Certificates
6. Consultations
7. Referral Cards
8. Websites
9. Social Posts
10. Newsletters
11. Team Brochures
12. Bundled Offers
13. Direct Mail
14. Patient Events
15. Sponsorships
16. Workshops
17. Podcasts
18. Video Interviews
19. Webinars
20. Referral Mixers
21. Charity Champion Campaigns

The power of social media to share your message with the masses is unreliable. As you review these co-marketing campaigns, consider outsourcing to a firm like ZLinked Marketing and Advertising which specializes in helping dental practices through "done-for-you" social media campaigns. With a partner such as ZLinked, social media becomes a strategic yet simple part of your program. Each week, they will create and post customized messages on Facebook, Instagram, Twitter, LinkedIn, Pinterest and Google. They even advertise your brand in a way that systematically incorporates social media at an extremely affordable price so have one less thing to worry about. ZLinked works collaboratively with your in-house team and web team so they can continue doing what they already do well. For more information on how affordable and simple outsourced social media solutions can be, visit:

https://zlinkedmarketing.com/.

1 - Introductions

When meeting with a new Referral Partner, an easy YES to get things moving is making introductions to other professionals you each know. After all, your new referral partner likely knows some great prospective partners for you. Can you imagine what life will be like when people start referring you their best clients who are a pleasure to work with when they become your patients. Think about the difference you will be able to make in other people's businesses when you share professionals you also work with. As we work together and cross-refer through our Referral Alliances, WE ALL WIN TOGETHER.

The reason to start with making introductions is that it is an easy ask you both should be very comfortable moving forward with. Starting the conversation by getting them to agree to something small will increase the likelihood they will agree on other campaigns later on.

Remember to give first. Start by suggesting a few people who you know might be good prospective partners for them. Tell them about each person and offer to introduce them. You might even want to set up a zoom or face-to-face meetings with the three of you so you can meet socially. Because dentistry has privacy laws to be mindful of, be sure introductions are only made when it is professional to professional and not patient to professional without permission from a patient.

The beauty about making introductions to people is that often as a result of your introduction these new alliances will think of you as a result of your introduction. The more introductions you make, the more often you are likely coming up in other people's conversations, which keeps you and your practice top of mind.

Once you've suggested a few introductions, the other person will likely offer some people they can introduce you to. This is where you want to make sure you communicate exactly what types of potential patients you want to be introduced to. The clearer you are, the more likely they are to connect you with quality patients who have the ability to also refer a lot of additional Perfect Prospects your way.

2 - Client Referrals

Next, we suggest you discuss referring each other to your respective clients. As you start sending each other new client opportunities, both partners win more business together. Again, start by giving first and mention that you have quite a few clients you can refer their way. If you have a referral, you can give them there and then, even better. The more you refer them, the more they will reciprocate.

Explain that as you build referral partnerships, you are always scouting and looking out for new clients you can introduce to your partners. If that sounds like something they are interested in, you would be happy to proactively refer them clients and hope they will do the same for you.

Then simply ask them how that sounds. Their response will tell you a lot. If they sound hesitant, they either may not be the right partner you are looking for, or they need time to get to know, like, and trust you more before committing to that level of alliance.

3 - Ratings and Reviews

Another way to help your referral partners boost their credibility and visibility is to give each other ratings or reviews on Google, Yelp, Angi's List, HOA.com, or any other sites and services where you each promote yourselves. Just ask your partner if they use ratings and reviews in their marketing and if they'd like you to give them a rating or review. You should also let them know which sites you are using and see if they'd be willing to give you a rating or review. You can even get it done right then before you end your meeting.

The importance of reviews cannot be overstated. Recently, was in New York City for a C-Suite Network event led by its charismatic

CEO Jeffrey Hayzlett. During the conference, I was talking with the SVP of Global Strategic Partnerships and Business Development for the Amazon company Audible. Helena shared that Audible now uses reviews as their top marketing strategy to drive revenue. Their testing shows member reviews are far more effective in attracting and retaining new subscribers. In the online world, reviews rule. If a tech giant like Audible who has done extensive marketing research believes in the power of reviews, so should you.

We humans trust the collective power of reviews because we feel like the research has been done for us. Again, people care far more what other people say about you than what you say about yourself. Especially when those people are high Blueprint or Knowledge personality types.

4 - Special Offers

Everyone loves to save money and get a deal. That's why offering special "partner only" discounts is another great way to help your partners promote your practice. This helps your partners give their clients something special and gives your partners an easy way to introduce your practice.

For dental practices, you can certainly offer free consults, x-rays, etc. But you might find by offering a VIP treatment or something unique from dentistry that you actually get more traction. Oftentimes it's that thing that hasn't been done that can get the most attention. We often see the same offers over and over and they truly are not unique. We see this on the windows of practices, in their ads, social media and more and they are the exact same as so many other practices.

Consider clever or unique ways of making the patient experience special for people. For example, rather than just offering a photo booth for selfies in your practice, consider featuring a hot local artist every month or quarter to create a destination experience. I know a popular dentist who turned two rooms of his practice into an art gallery for a local college and held monthly art openings to feature the student artists. When coming up with special offers, think outside the box.

5 - Gift Certificates

There's no better price than free. That's why gift certificates are the ultimate way to package your special offer. Gift certificates allow your partners to recommend your services by giving their clients and customers something with high perceived value. While you may not want to give away your products and services for free, you can package a discount as a gift certificate to boost the perceived value. For example, if your average service costs $100, giving a $25 gift certificate is essentially a 25% discount.

Gift certificates work especially well for new homeowners moving into communities surrounding your office. Consider printing special "Welcome to the neighborhood" gift certificates you give away through your Realtor and mortgage lender patients and referral partners.

After moving into a new neighborhood, studies show that 85% of homeowners choose to use the first company they come into contact with. So shouldn't that be your dental practice. Giving real estate agents your gift certificates to give to their buyers as part of their closing gift is a win for the homeowner, for the Realtor and for you.

Examples of gift certificates include:

- Free Teeth Whitening
- Free Initial Exam & X-Rays
- Free Invisalign Exam
- Free Orthodontics Assessment & SmileView Simulator
- Free Dental Implant Consultation
- Free Apple iWatch for New Ortho Patients
- $100 Gift Certificate for New Patients
- $250 Gift Certificate for Clear Aligners

- $500 Cosmetic Dentistry Gift Certificate
- $1,000 Gift Certificate for Full Arch Implants

Simply print your gift certificates and include a brochure or flier on your services for your referral partners to give to their clients. You may even want to have special gift certificate envelopes printed to create a special impression for your new clients. Just be sure to check with your attorney or state dental association to ensure you are compliant with all state regulations.

6 - Consultations

If you provide free consultations for your new patient process, encourage your referral partner to include you as part of theirs. Giving their clients a free consultation makes your referral partner look good and provides value to everyone involved.

Offering a free consultation is also a great way to capture qualified potential patients that actually want to switch to your practice. Not only do consultations help you capture more referrals, but you can streamline your conversion process and add massive value by demonstrating your expertise and generosity in advance.

Consider creating a special landing page on your website or printing gift certificates or brochures that describe the service you provide to your partner's clients. Place a value on the assessment so the client understands they are getting something special thanks to your referral partner.

7 - Referral Cards

If you want to attract more Raving Referrals, it is imperative you make it easy for people to refer you. The fastest way to accomplish that is by giving people printed referral cards they can quickly hand to anyone who may need a new dentist. This also helps you track where your business is coming from so you can recognize and reward your referrers.

You have probably received a referral card from your chiropractor, or home services professional. They are an inexpensive and effective way to help people help you. By including all the essential referral program information, these cards provide a simple way for people to refer others to your business.

One of the simplest ways to add a referral card into your business is by adding your referral offer to the back of your existing business card. You can also print a special postcard size promotional piece that gives people details about your product or service along with a special offer.

Consider using a bookmark or coaster in lieu of a business card to be more memorable. Again, try something different so others remember you. If you're going to invest in a way to promote, make sure it does the job and doesn't get thrown out in the trash.

Be sure to include a catchy headline or slogan like:

- Share a smile
- Refer a friend
- Help us spread the word
- Sharing is caring
- Friends wanted
- Pass it on
- A gift for you and your friends

Below the headline, include a call to action that gives people a reward for taking action. Offer a discount, free consultation, or special offer to make them feel special and increase the number of people who take advantage of your offer.

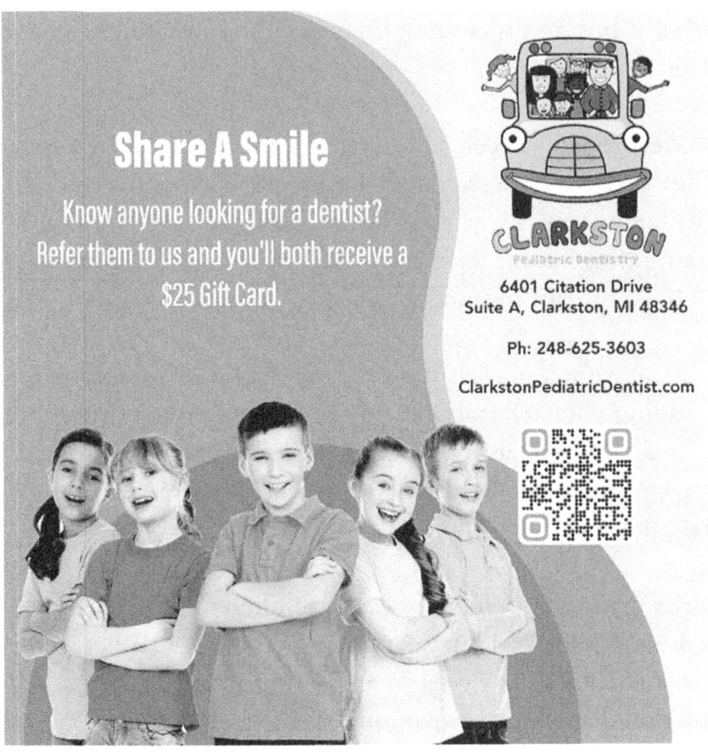

Affordable Dental Implants

We Love Referrals

Call us at

602-932-7773

to schedule your free consultation.

AriaDentalImplantCenter.com

12320 N. 32nd St. STE #3, Phoenix, AZ 85032

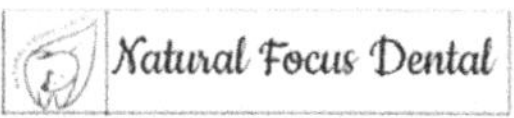

QUALITY
AFFORDABLE
DENTAL CARE

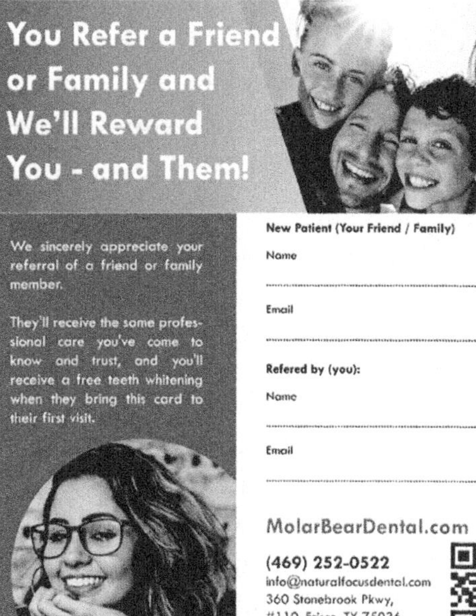

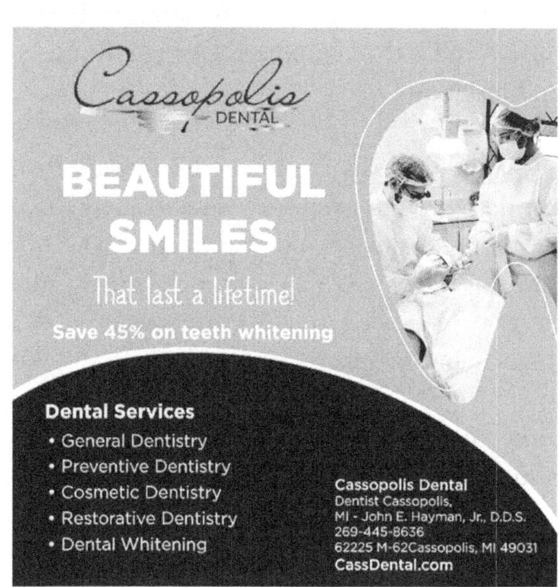

8 - Websites

Another great way to cross promote with your partners is by adding and recommencing them on your respective websites. Simply add them to a page that lists your resources, trusted partners, or preferred providers with links to their website or social media pages. Create a page on your site where your clients and customers can explore and connect with your trusted team of referral partners.

When creating a referral partner page of your website, list each partner with a sentence or two about the services they offer.

Display their contact information including phone number and website URL. Include their logo or banner ad linked to their website. If your partner offers special pricing or promotions, position that prominently so people know you are helping them unlock special pricing or treatment. You may also want to add a testimonial or success story from one of your patients. Years ago, my company was a Preferred Supplier for Prudential Real Estate Affiliates, which was later purchased and rebranded as Berkshire Hathaway Home Services. Being listed on their website brought instant credibility to our company and led to hundreds of their Realtors joining our online referral program.

While many of their agents found us through the listing on their global Prudential corporate website, we also used the endorsement as a strategic partner when marketing to their agents directly. The credibility and visibility you gain when partners promote you on their website can be significant. Especially when you partner with influential brands and people.

Consider some of the recognizable companies and names within your community that you could co-brand with. You'd be surprised how much a name can uplevel your credibility and recognizability in a community.

9 - Social Posts

Social media is a powerful way to cross-promote with your partners. It's fast, easy, and free. When you combine forces and collaborate on Facebook, Instagram, Twitter, TikTok or LinkedIn, you reach new audiences creating instant credibility through the exposure and endorsement from your partner.

The key to this strategy is to coordinate a conversation by posting publicly. This creates an opportunity for your referral partners to answer, comment, and create a dialogue that others see and participate in. We recommend you pre-plan or at least coordinate what you and your partners are going to post so that both parties are promoted and provide value to your respective tribes of clients, fans, and followers. Some of the most effective ways to co-market with your partners include:

- Success Stories – Thank your partner publicly for helping clients get great results. Share the thanks you received from your clients for introducing your referral partners.
- Testimonials – Share your personal story of how impressed you've been by their knowledge, professionalism, and expertise. If you've personally used their product or service, share that as well to build social proof and trust.
- Expert Content – Provide special reports or whitepapers that educate people.
- Special Offers – Post discounts, promotions, or special offers.
- Events – Invite people to attend online or in-person events with you and your partners.
- Questions and Quizzes – Post questions about your partners industry or area of expertise, tagging them to respond.
- Photos and Videos – Show before and after photos or videos to give visual examples of the impact you make.
- Go Live – Have a social conversation for the world to watch about anything from the list above.

10 - Newsletters

If you send out printed or email newsletters to your patients and prospect database, consider adding a section for your Referral Partners or top trusted pros. This adds value to your referral partners and shows you are committed to helping them win more clients. As you lead the partnership, they will feel indebted and want to return the favor either by giving you referrals directly or by cross-promoting you to their networks and social sphere. Just be sure to ask if they send out newsletters to their client list or database. If so, you can use any of the strategies above to cross- promote with your partners.

11 - Team Brochures

As you start creating your trusted team of professionals, consider printing brochures featuring you and each of your referral partners. This gives both you and your partners a physical marketing tool you can share with your patients and display in your lobby. If you use this strategy, be sure all of the partners make a habit of giving these out to each new client so everyone in your referral team is continuously promoting each other.

Team brochures work extremely well when you have a core group of professionals serving a specific target market or life event. Simply write an introduction as to the joint services and solution your team provides. Then list each partner including their name, company, logo, phone number, and website address. You may also want to include a brief statement or bulleted list of the specific services each partner provides.

12 - Bundled Offers

Another way to cross promote your partners is to actually bundle their services with your own. The way this strategy works is that you and your referral partner combine your services into one integrated solution or offer at a bundled price. You probably see this with travel companies who bundle airfare, hotel, car rental, and excursions into one bundled package. Mobile phone companies often bundle short-term subscriptions to music or movie applications with the purchase of a new phone in order to entice buyers and add extra value.

You just have to think creatively on how you can share your services with each other's audiences. The more ways that you and your referral partners scout for new client and patient opportunities for each other, the more business you will all have.

13 - Direct Mail

Once you are in agreement with your referral partners on a special offer, bundled service, or joint promotion you want to offer, sending your campaign through direct mail is a great way to get the word out. It gives your respective clients something tangible they can touch and feel forcing them to view your message and offer. When you utilize referred introductions and bundled offers into your direct mail campaign, you can leverage and maximize the results for both you and your referral partners.

While you may choose to mail your joint campaign to your respective lists, you can also purchase or rent a list of Perfect Prospects you share with your partners. This allows you and your partners to target people in transitionary life events.

There are several top life events that cause people to search out new service professionals which you can target through direct mail campaigns including:

- New Homeowners
- Engaged or Just Married
- Expecting or New Parents
- Retiring or Recently Retired
- Divorcing or Recently Divorced
- Moving or Recently Moved

14 - Client Celebration Events

Events are a great way to bring people together and create new opportunities to connect. Consider hosting a quarterly or annual patient celebration event with your referral partners. This can be as simple as hosting a happy hour at your office, or a local restaurant, bar, or hotel.

What's great about hosting these types of events with your referral partners is you can expand your audience while having fun celebrating great people. The key is to communicate to your referral partners the type of clients or professionals you would like them to invite so they fill the room with your perfect prospects.

As a reminder, some of the patient appreciation events you can produce with your referral partners include:

- Art Showings
- Awards Parties: Oscars, Grammy 's, Golden Globes
- Bowling Parties
- Casino Nights
- Charity Fundraising Events
- Cigar Nights
- Concerts
- Cornhole Tournaments
- Golf Tournaments
- Holiday Parties: Valentine's Day, Independence Day, Halloween, Thanksgiving, Christmas, New Year's Eve
- Private Movie Showings
- Sporting Events
- Top Golf Tournaments
- Wine Tours and Tasting

Be sure to capture everyone's contact information so you can follow up with them after the event to explore a relationship together.

15 - Sponsorships

If your referral partners already produce or participate in their own training events or conferences, you may want to consider sponsoring or exhibiting at their events. This shows your partners you support them and are committed to helping them achieve success. Sponsorship also creates opportunities for your referral partners to introduce or promote you and your services to their clients and strategic partners.

You'll be amazed how many other partnership opportunities present themselves when you support your partners. The more you show up to help your partners in their passions and pursuits, the more they will recommend you and your practice.

In addition to sponsoring existing referral partners, you may want to sponsor:

- Association Events
- Bridal Expos
- Business Expos
- Chamber Of Commerce Events
- Charity Events
- Community Events
- Concerts
- Conferences
- Golf Tournaments
- Home And Garden Expos
- Networking Events
- Podcasts
- Races
- School Carnivals
- Sporting Events
- Trade Shows
- Webinars
- Websites

When considering a sponsorship opportunity, look to maximize exposure to your Perfect Patients. If the event sponsor is gathering your ideal patients, the return on investment may justify the opportunity, especially since many event promoters will provide you the database of attendees as part of your sponsorship package.

Sponsorship benefits you should ask for include:

- Award Presentations
- Banner Ads on The Event Website and Mobile App
- Brochures Or Samples included in Attendee Gift Bags
- Direct Mail Campaigns
- Email Promotions before and after the Event
- Exhibitor Booth Space
- Logo Placement in Attendee Gift Bags
- Press Release
- Product Placement throughout the Event
- Signage throughout the Event
- Social Media Promotion
- Speaking Opportunities
- Tabletop Promotion
- VIP Sessions

16 - Workshops

As we discussed in chapter 11, workshops are a great way to educate people about the services you provide and the value you deliver. That's why you should talk to your partners about putting on a seminar, workshop, or lunch-and-learn training for your combined clients with each of you delivering a portion of the content. Just identify the top tips people need to know about the challenges you solve and how you help.

Training events help you attract qualified clients and boost your status as experts in your field. Once people have attended your class, they will understand why they need your service, and how you can help them solve their challenges and overcome their obstacles.

By establishing your expertise, you instantly elevate your status. Especially to those guests invited by your partners. There's simply no better way to gain the credibility and trust that gets transferred from the introduction of your referral partners. Plus, by mutually promoting the event to your respective clients, patients, customers, fans, and followers, you leverage your combined audience to attract more profitable prospects.

If you produce the event and get your referral partners to promote it to their lists, you can expand your prospect database by capturing the contact information for all the people who register for the event. Then you can follow up with a variety of offers using your CRM or follow up system.

17 - Podcasts

Podcasts have grown in popularity and are now one of the best ways to establish yourself as an expert. Similar to a live work- shop, podcasts give you an opportunity to interview your referral partners on their area of expertise.

The strategy works just like a workshop, except rather than producing an in-person event, you simply record and broadcast your conversation much like a radio interview. Then you can post the audio file for people to listen to on their mobile device or computer. This allows them to download and listen to your conversation when it's most convenient for them.

Podcasts give you valuable content that both you and your referral partners can give away to prospects. You can also transcribe the recording and produce a special report your clients and social sphere can benefit from. The beauty of this strategy is that your referral partners will be happy to share the recording with their network because you are helping them boost their status and showcase their expertise.

Just imagine how many referrals and leads you will attract when you get the right partners to promote your podcast to their audience because you have made them the star of the show.

Be sure to ask for a bio or some background on your referral partner so you can introduce them effectively. You may also want to research them on LinkedIn, their website, or social media to identify some interesting information to include in your conversation.

Here are some great questions you can ask during your podcast:

- How did you get started in your industry?
- What are the biggest challenges people come to you with?
- What is the most important thing you hope people learn from our conversation today?
- What would you say are the most common myths people have about your industry?
- What are some specific warning signs people should watch out for in your industry?
- What are you most proud of in your business?
- What are you most passionate about?
- Outside of work, what do you spend your time doing?
- What charities or social causes are you most passionate about?
- How has social media changed the way you do business?
- In your opinion, what is the future of…?
- How is technology impacting your industry?
- Tell me something that's true that almost nobody agrees with you on.
- How can people learn more about you and the solutions you provide?
- What's the best way for our listeners to connect with you?

We always recommend you give first and offer to interview your referral partners on your own podcast. This activates the law of reciprocity and will often lead them to return the favor. This strategy works powerfully when you interview people who already have significant social followings. Once the interview is over, offer to help them further by allowing them to interview you.

Just say, *"By the way, if it would be helpful, I would be happy to have you interview me so you have some content you can share with your audience."* You will find they will be happy to return the favor, especially because they now feel indebted to you.

18 - Video Interviews

While audio podcasts are quick and easy to produce, video interviews via zoom and going live on social media are great ways to educate audiences about who and how you help. Before your interview, ask your partner what topics they want to cover and if they have any specific questions they would like you to ask. Then you can talk about the problems they solve and the solutions they provide.

Again, make sure they give you some background information so you can introduce them properly and establish their credibility. To prepare your partner, ask them to identify top tips people should know about their subject. This will give them confidence going into the interview and help you guide the conversation. Then ask the questions you've agreed to beforehand and invite any live viewers to ask any questions they have.

The video itself doesn't have to be a major Hollywood production. It can be a simple video shot on your mobile phone. Just do some testing and make sure the camera is steady, the lighting is good, and the audio is loud enough for your audience to hear clearly. You can shoot the video at one of your offices or out at a jobsite. If you can show visual examples of the work your referral partner does, even better.

Your goal is to give great content that helps your audience solve their challenges. Include a call to action at the end that makes it clear how to contact you and your referral partners should the person have questions or want to move forward.

19 - Webinars

Another way to present your expertise and attract clients for both you and your referral partners is by offering online webinars. The beauty of webinars is you can educate your audience and present your solutions far and wide. You can give presentations, perform product demonstrations, and deliver worldwide messages to thousands of people at a time. And if you create content that is informative and inspirational, you'll get great results and build a large list of prospects for your respective follow-up funnels.

Plus, because webinars are virtual, they save people from having to travel to attend your training in person and help you avoid the considerable costs of paying for meals or conference rooms to host live physical events.

To maximize the success of your webinar, follow these 10 steps:

1. Choose a Topic – Identify a topic that points out the pain points of your perfect prospects to inspire them to register for your training.
2. Choose a Date and Time – Select a time that works well for people locally and nationally if appropriate.
3. Choose a Webinar Platform – GoToWebinar, Zoom, and WebinarJam are the platforms I've used and personally recommend.
4. Invite Your Audience – Both partners should text and email their databases and promote the event on your websites, blogs, and social media accounts.

5. Build Your Content – Create slides that identify the challenges you solve and spotlight the solutions and expertise each partner delivers.
6. Practice – Be sure to do a quick test run to ensure you're comfortable with the technology and that both speakers know which slides or sections each will be presenting.
7. Host and Record Your Webinar – Present your webinar as a masterclass, panel discussion, interview, case study, or product demo. Be sure to record it so you can post and share afterwards.
8. Ask For Action – Have a compelling call-to-action asking attendees to buy, try, or schedule a consultation to learn more.
9. Follow-Up – After your event, be sure to email, text, message, or call everyone who attended as well as those who registered but did not attend.
10. Share Your Webinar Recording – Post your webinar recording on your social media channels and email to your prospect and client database. You can even add the video to your website to provide ongoing education for your audience.

Some people choose to charge for their webinars, but if you're looking to attract a larger audience and build your prospect database, you should offer your class for free. This will give you the largest prospect list to follow up with after the webinar.

While you can sell products and services directly during your webinars, many people use webinars more to educate prospects who schedule a private consultation. Just be sure people feel the pain of not taking action, so they are motivated to move forward and learn more about the solutions you provide.

Landing the right promotional partner for your webinars can lead to hundreds or even thousands of Perfect Prospects being added to your sales funnel. One of our recent webinar campaigns attracted over 5,000 webinar registrants over a two-week period with over 2,000 people joining our live class. Rather than having to rent a conference center and incur the costs of producing an event of that size, we were able to host our event virtually which made it easy for everyone to attend.

20 - Referral Mixers

Hosting Referral Mixers is a fun and effective way to meet high quality professionals and prospects. When you host mixers, you become the central connector elevating your status as the leader of the group. Asking your top referral partners to co-host mixers helps you add value to your referral partners while you create a community of high-quality professionals.

Mixers provide the opportunity for people to meet in a festive and friendly atmosphere. Your role is simply to meet and introduce the people in your tribe. The more you help other people make new connections, the more your own network will grow.

This can easily be coordinated either at your office or a nearby restaurant, hotel, bar, or golf course. Once you know the location, date and time, you can start promoting the event using email, Eventbrite, Evite, a Facebook event, or other event invitation system. Then, enlist your referral partners to help get the word out by inviting their clients along with top professionals they know, like, and trust.

You can even target the event for a certain industry or group of professionals. Just be specific with your referral partners letting them know the types of people you are looking to attract so they fill the event with your Perfect Prospects. Then, when your mixer starts, you get to meet every single person who walks in the door as they check in at the registration table.

Best of all, you are meeting them from a position of prominence. You'll find them grateful for the invitation and impressed to meet the event producer bringing together so many fabulous people. The more you position yourself as a connector and catalyst, the more people will seek you out, asking how they can earn your trust and win your business.

If you live in a major market, you can always plug into existing networking events like those produced by Network After Work. They host events in over 80 major US markets typically bringing together over a hundred prominent professionals to each event. Strategically invite your referral partners to attend these events together with you. You will both increase your connections as you work the room together and introduce prospective referral partners and Perfect Prospects to each other.

21 - Charity Champion Campaigns

Personally, I love to partner with people to support charities and causes. You don't need to create your own charity to tap into the power of cause-related marketing. You can simply raise awareness, funds, and support for great causes and charities already doing good work.

Ask your referral partner if they have any charities or causes, they support. If so, discuss how you might join forces and create more awareness and support for the causes that are near and dear to them. If you have a charity or organization, you are passionate about, suggest that your referral partner join forces so you can create more impact together.

Some of the most fun and inspiring cause related marketing campaigns I've produced over the years include:

- Christmas Kindness – We produced a Christmas drive collecting toys, clothing, and canned food culminating with a concert and community celebration in Pioneer Square, the community courtyard in the center of downtown Portland. We gave points for each donation and awarded the top donation raiser a one-week trip to Cabo San Lucas, Mexico.

- Virtual Veteran Salute – We created VirtualSalute.com to honor U.S. veterans helping people nationwide post photos and stories honoring the veterans in their lives.
- We've Been Booed – A fun and festive community-based campaign to spread joy before Halloween.
- Donate Profit or Revenue – One of my training companies donated 40% of our gross sales to charity partners who provided food, water, education and microloans in developing nations.
- Empowerment Trainings – We sent a volunteer team to lead the single largest private teacher training in the African nation of Liberia with the nation's President commencing over the day event.
- Voluntour Trips – We led volunteer teams overseas in Mexico and Africa as well as to South Dakota to build infrastructure for a Native American reservation.
- Water Wells – We helped drill water wells in Kenya.
- Food Drives – We helped produce the largest single food donation distribution day in the city of Los Angeles in partnership with Feed the Children led by Larry Jones and NBA legend Shaquille O'Neal.
- Candle Wishes – We supported a charity that provides birthday parties and gifts for underprivileged kids.
- Toys For Tots – We collected and donated toys for kids at Christmas.
- Super V Pumpkin Shoot – We created a 2-day competition hurling pumpkins hundreds of yards using roman catapults with all proceeds donated to Northwest Medical Teams.
- Dog Rescues – We regularly shelter, transport, and help dogs get rescued and adopted in the U.S. and Mexico.

These are some of my favorite give-back campaigns that have brought immense joy to me, my family, my employees, and my referral partners. While the business benefits are great, the personal satisfaction you get when you make a difference in the lives of others is immeasurable. There's simply nothing better than being a Charity Champion.

Each event creates an opportunity to invite your referral partners to participate and collaborate. Plus, when they see you as a leader committed to improving your community, they will want to do business with you for years to come. Whether you donate your time, talent, money, or promotion, everyone wins. Do more and give more for others and your life will be richly rewarded.

It Works When You Work It

These are the top 21 cross promotion campaigns you should consider implementing in your practice. Hopefully you now see how using the *Referral Partner Blueprint* in your meetings with prospective and existing referral partners will help you have highly productive meetings that lead to profitable partnerships.

As you review each of the strategies, you will quickly gain clarity and agreement on what each person is willing to do for the other. Then as you put these 21 proven co-marketing campaigns to work in your practice, you and your referral partners will be thrilled as you attract more opportunities together.

Keep it simple. Start with the easiest campaigns you both feel most comfortable with and confident in. Then as you start seeing results and attracting more profitable prospects, you can implement additional co-marketing campaigns down the road at a later date.

Agree On Your Plan

As you and your referral partners sit down and create your *Referral Partner Blueprint*, be sure to agree on:

1. What each person will promote
2. When each partner will promote
3. How often each partner will promote

Print our handy checklist to use in your referral partner meetings. This will guide your conversation with prospective partners and help you both strategize the various ways you will cross promote each other.

Once your *Referral Partner Blueprint* is in place and you have agreed how each person or company will promote and refer the other, simply do what you committed to do, by the time you committed to do it, while your partner does the same.

Then, as the leads and new client opportunities start rolling in, be sure to thank them each and every time they generate another prospect for you. Provide regular updates on the status of each client they refer to you, so they know exactly how you are helping each of their clients. This will lead them to refer more clients because their appreciation for you will grow quickly.

As we mentioned earlier, referral updates display a high level of professionalism, which continually build trust and will lead to further collaboration and opportunities together.

Your mutual clients will also tell your referral partners about how you've helped them. As your partners share success stories with other clients facing similar challenges, you will attract even more Raving Referrals for you and your firm.

Once you and your partners start actively referring and cross-promoting each other, you will find that your referrals and bottom-line profits will increase steadily. You'll also develop some deep meaningful relationships with people you are proud to call your friends.

Co-marketing with your partners helps expand the visibility of your brand and the loyalty of your partners.

Scan this QR code or visit the link below for a quick video
on how to get your message out to the masses
through partners who proactively promote you to
their best clients, customers, and social sphere:

https://ravingreferrals.com/comarketing/

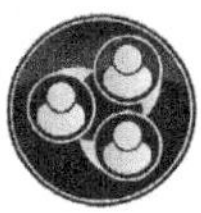

Chapter 17

Take ACTION To WIN

You are now empowered with the strategies, scripts, tips, and tricks you need to succeed. Everything you hope to accomplish can be achieved using the knowledge and wisdom you have in your hands. My question to you is, will you take the ACTION you need to win big?

The key to activating the Law of Attraction is taking MASSIVE ACTION. The more ACTION you take, the faster your practice will grow. The good news is you can easily integrate what you've learned into your daily activities. With a few tweaks to what you already do, you can easily and effortlessly attract more Perfect Prospects and ideal clients.

As you start receiving Raving Referrals, we want to hear from you. Please take a moment and share your success story on our social channels. We'll reward you with a super-secret gift you'll be thrilled to receive.

We'd Love to Partner with You

Our team at The Champions Institute has helped hundreds of dental practices grow their business which is exactly why we created our Champion Dentists program. The beauty of our pay-for-performance dental consulting and coaching program is that our compensation is earned on actual performance, not promises. This win-win program is delivered through a no-risk partnership agreement where you only pay after you experience results, and your revenue rises.

Whether your goal is to increase new patient attraction, boost your case acceptance, or optimize your staff retention and loyalty, our Champion Dentists program has been designed to maximize the valuation of your dental business.

Our productivity program uses a proprietary, process-driven, systematic approach to identify, evaluate and address key opportunities to boost your results. We use an advanced methodology that helps you generate lasting results increasing both your gross revenue and net profit quickly and consistently.

Become A Champion Dentist Today!

Our Champion Dentists program helps you operate your dental practice at the highest level of performance and profitability. Those lucky enough to be chosen for this elite performance-based coaching and consulting program learn to elevate all aspects of operating your dental business. We teach you and your team a proven leadership methodology to help your practice build a "Championship Culture" that elevates the performance, productivity, happiness and loyalty of your staff.

We invite you to schedule a complimentary profit optimization assessment call today to see how much additional revenue your practice is capable of.

Call us at 888-906-2070
or visit https://ChampionDentists.com.

Success Scripts

Scripts for Generating Raving Referrals

The following call and conversation scripts have been refined over decades of testing. Our goal is to give your clarity and confidence to help you generate Raving Referrals and profitable partnerships.

Whether you choose to make these calls yourself or train your team to lead your referral partnership and business development campaign, these scripts will save you time and boost productivity by avoiding the learning curve we've gone through over the years. Do your best to customize your conversations based on each person's **BANK**CODE to accelerate your results even faster.

Scripts or Building Referral Partnerships:

Hi (name), the reason I'm calling is that I'm creating a team of professionals I'll be recommending to my patients and colleagues. I was thinking about you because I have a lot of patients who could benefit from your services. I'd love to sit down with you to discuss the possibility of adding you to my team and promoting you. When's a good time to get together and strategize?

Thanks so much for your time today. I'd like to ask for your help. As you may know, I am in the process of expanding my practice and I'm looking for a great CPA to refer my patients to, so I'm wondering if you know of any good CPAs you think I should meet. I'm planning to meet and interview 2-3 and your CPA will be one of those I would like to meet with. Not just for my personal business, but also for the opportunity to refer clients to them. Is there anyone you'd recommend I meet with?

Stephen really sounds like an interesting person I would love to meet. Would you mind introducing the two of us? Or, if you would prefer, I am happy to send an email and mention you had great things to say about them and I would like to get to know them myself.

Thanks so much for the introduction. Would you be willing to make a quick call or send them a text to tell them how we know each other and that I will be calling them (date & time of scheduled call)? Is there anything you think I should know before I call them?

Thanks for meeting with me today. I've heard a lot of great things about you. You come highly recommended. The reason I wanted to meet with you is that I serve a lot of (type of people – homeowners/ business owners) who may be able to use your services. I'm hoping to learn more about you and your business so I'm referring you the right type of clients."

I'm glad to hear referrals are important to you. I work almost exclusively by referral which is exactly why I am here today. As I mentioned earlier, I'm looking for quality people I can partner with to grow our businesses together. Based on what you shared about your business, you are definitely the type of person I'm looking to add to my trusted team of professionals that I promote and refer my patients and colleagues to.

Just to give you a little more background on me....

From what you've shared, I have a number of patients who might benefit from what you do. Can we get together another time so I can ask you a few questions? Maybe next Tuesday afternoon or Wednesday morning? What works best for you?

Hope all is well in your world. I'm reaching out because I am looking to expand my professional network and noticed you are connected to a few people on LinkedIn that I'd like to meet. I have a few contacts I think you would benefit from meeting as well. Do you have a few minutes to jump on a quick call so we can connect and collaborate? What day and time works best for your schedule?

Hi (name), As you may know, I am in the process of expanding my practice and I'm creating an alliance of vetted and trusted professionals to refer my clients to. I truly value our relationship and would like to invite you to be a core member of my referral team. I will be gathering my most important referral partners (date/time) at (location) and hope you can attend. Please let me know if you can join us.

Referral Partner Alliance Meeting Script:

Thank you for coming today. The reason I asked you all to join me today is that I am expanding my practice and I'm creating an alliance of vetted and trusted professionals to refer my clients to.

I truly value each and every one of you and view you as one of the best in your respective industries. Not only am I hoping to do more business with you personally, I also want to connect each of you so you can do more business together.

After all, everyone in this room serves (consumers, homeowners, business owners), so we share the same ideal client/patients and can grow our businesses faster and further by cross-referring and cross-promoting each other.

What I'd like to do now is go around the room and give everyone a chance to introduce themselves and share who you help and how you help. That will help us all understand the services you provide and who your perfect prospects and ideal clients are.

I'll go first. As you all know, my name is ________________, and I help {share your Service Statement}.

To give you an example of what I do, I recently had a client who ____________________. {share a story of a problem you solved and the difference it made for them}.

I'm passionate about helping people ____________ and a great referral for me is a {share your Perfect Prospect Profile}.

Before we move on, does anyone have any questions about the services I provide?

By the way, if it would be helpful, I would be happy to have you interview me so you have some content you can share with your clients/network/audience.

Scripts for Networking Events

The main reason I am here is that I'm looking for a quality (CPA) I can refer my clients to. Do you happen to know any good (CPA)s here you would recommend I connect with?

I'm wondering if you can help me. The primary reason I'm here is to find a top (CPA) that I can refer patients and colleagues to and build a referral partnership with. Can you tell me if there are any quality (CPA)'s here I can connect with?

By the way, if you ever have a friend or family member you think might benefit from my services, I would be happy to meet with them at no charge to see how I might be able to help them.

Scripts to Activate the Referral Triggers

I hope you're pleased with the service I've provided so far. Is there anything I can do to make you even happier?

Now that we've been working together for a while, I'm wondering if you can tell me what you have found most valuable about working with me?

I'm committed to growing my practice through exceptional service. On a scale of 1-10, how happy would you say you are with my services?

Do you mind if I ask what you have liked best about working with me?

Thanks for sharing your feedback. Before you go, I'd like to ask you, if someone you know was asking about me or the services I provide, what would you tell them?

If you don't mind me asking, if you knew someone who was looking for a *{insert your profession}* how likely would you be to recommend me? What would you say?

Scripts to use when you hear the Referral Triggers

I'm so glad to hear that. I hope you'll recommend me any time you hear any *{describe your Perfect Patient/Prospect}* mention that they are looking for a good dentist or need help *{share your Service Statement}*. Is there anyone who comes to mind who might need my help?

I'm so glad you feel that way. I love helping people like you

{share your Service Statement}. By the way, I may have mentioned before that I am expanding my practice so if you know any *{describe your Perfect Prospect}* who might need help *{share your Service Statement},* I'd love to connect with them and see if I can help them the way I helped you?

Do you know anyone who is looking *to {share your Service Statement}?*

Scripts for Asking Clients for Referrals

Thanks for meeting with me today. Before you leave, I'd like to ask for your help. As you may know, I am in the process of expanding my practice and one of the ways I keep my costs down is by working primarily by referral, so I don't have to spend much time or money on advertising. Once I've taken care of you and hopefully have exceeded your expectations, I'd like to ask your permission to ask you for referrals. Would that be all right?

As you may know, I prefer working with people who are referred to us. Right now, I'm giving a special discount to friends or family of our existing clients. If there's anyone you'd like to refer to me, they will get an extra 10% off our premier package (customize with your offer). And of course, I'll take extra special care of them since they're coming from you. Is there anyone you can think of who might like to take advantage of this?

As you know, nearly all of my patients come from referrals. A good referral for me is {describe your Perfect Patient/Prospect} who might need help {share your Service Statement}. Of everyone you know, who would be the best referral for me? Why do you say that?

As you know, nearly all of my patients come from referrals. I'm hoping we can brainstorm for a few minutes to see if we can identify some people you care about who should at least know about the work we do and how we help people. Would that be alright?

Great. Please let me know if there's anyone you know I can help. I'm always here for you and your clients.

Congratulations on completing the Raving Referrals book.

You now have the proven strategies, scripts, tips, and tricks you need to succeed.

Scan this QR code on the following page or visit the link below for a quick video on the #1 most important driver for success in attracting Raving Referrals:

https://ravingreferrals.com/completion/

Recommended Resources

As a dental professional, you are always looking for the most advanced and beneficial dental products, services, and training. That's why we have researched and compiled a list of recommended resources to help you elevate the quality of care you provide and optimize the productivity and profitability of your practice.

3D Implant Institute

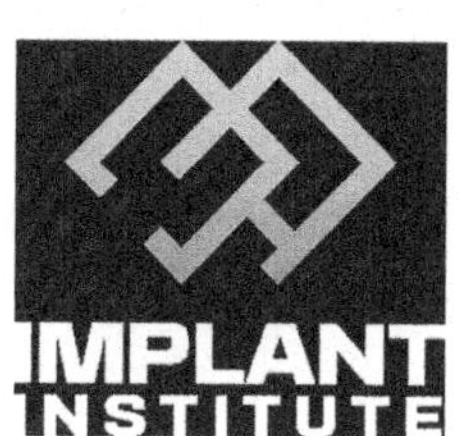

3D Implant Institute is designed to promote exceptional skills to surgeons who wish to acquire superior dental implant techniques. Our faculty have extensive implant experience and are experts in educating you with the latest innovations and ethical models. This intensive live surgery is limited to eighteen clinicians and gives you the opportunity and confidence to practice innovative approaches to bone regeneration, tissue engineering, sinus lift techniques, implant placement, and other surgical procedures. Patients are pre-selected with various levels of surgical complexity to match your clinical skills. All surgeries are performed at the free dental clinic. All participants receive temporary work permits from the Mexican Department of Health. Participants can place between 10 to 20 implants depending on the complexity of the cases and doctor's skill level. We hope you will join us in our mission to improve the quality of life for our patients and benefit from this unique opportunity.

https://3dImplantInstitute.com

3D Infusion Dental Training

3D Infusion Dental Training offers a "Hands On" technology integration training designed to strengthen your skills and build a better practice through planning, design and execution. With large open training areas, 3D Infusion is taking dental training into another dimension. This provides for a unique, experience-centered environment in a contemporary creative loft setting. It is through their community-based instruction and peer-to-peer training that they accommodate both doctors and their teams for simultaneous training. This high-touch personal approach to training allows doctors to gain great comfort levels with the emerging technology giving you the confidence to increase utilization. While the doctor is training on procedures, the team is learning the optimal workflow to help the doctor maximize his use of technology and time. This critical element is missing from most training, but 3D Infusion knows that a doctor can only be successful if their team is familiar with the technology and can properly support them in its implementation and use.

https://3dInfusionDental.com

3M Oral Care

Named most innovative company in the dental industry worldwide for 10 consecutive years, 3M products offer dental professionals' predictability and control for optimized patient outcomes. 3M Oral Care promotes lifelong oral health by developing innovative dental and orthodontic solutions that help simplify your procedures and give you confidence in your work. With a history of leadership in the dental and orthodontic industries and a scientific approach to product development, they create the high quality, advanced products you need to keep your patients smiling.

https://3m.com/3M/en_US/oral-care-us/

4M Institute

4M INSTITUTE

The 4M Institute provides cutting-edge progressive training to dentists to help you offer your patients the most advanced and appropriate care possible, while increasing your earning potential and adding value to your practice(s). When you train at 4M Institute, you are getting the best post-graduate, advanced education available; from leading techniques and state-of-the-art equipment, to the best trainers and highest tech institution. You learn not only how to perform same day, full-arch restorations, but how to market it to bring in patients now. With a focus on full-arch practices, 4M Institute is a leader in continuing dental training for everything from NeoArch to IV-Sedation, PFR/Phlebotomy and courses for your assistants. 4M Institute also provides leadership, sales and marketing training including the importance of PPC advertising, how powerful branding attracts patients, and how to track your marketing efforts.

https://4mInstitute.com

Academy of Oral Surgery

The Academy of Oral Surgery (AOS) is passionate about providing a pathway for practicing dentists and their team members to obtain the education and training necessary to successfully perform and complete procedures beyond what was taught to them in Dental School with the competence and confidence to provide the best care to their patients. The AOS focuses on instruction from well-qualified and experienced instructors who teach all aspects of oral surgery that are important for success.

Appropriate anatomy, biology, and preferred techniques are taught, and simple surgical procedures are mastered before more advanced ones are attempted. They focus on helping you avoid and manage complications with rare assistance, staying within the boundaries of your education and training, and knowing which cases should be treated by a specialist, or in cooperation with a specialist.

https://OralSurg.org

A-dec

For over 50 years, A-dec has been a recognized leader in manufacturing reliable dental operatory equipment. A-dec offers a variety of superior equipment including dental chairs, delivery systems, infection control, lights, stools, cabinets, and air purification systems. Their company has received numerous awards and accolades for their leadership and community impact.

https://A-Dec.com

Air Techniques

Air Techniques, Inc continues to pave the way with compelling, reliable dental products, ensuring today's dental professionals are "Equipped for Life®". With a strong product portfolio of utility systems, digital imaging and merchandise, Air Techniques products are capable of equipping the smallest practice to the largest university or hospital. From digital radiography, intraoral sensors, cameras, x-ray systems, air compressors, vacuum systems, infection prevention nitrous oxide and more, Air Techniques offers superior quality products and is a trusted brand to dealers and dental professionals worldwide.

https://AirTechniques.com

Align Technology

Famous for their game changing Invisalign® system, Align Technology has helped create millions of straighter smiles since their inception in 1997. By combining digital treatment planning and mass-customization, with shape-engineering based on biomechanical principles, they have revolutionized the orthodontic industry. Their database of approximately 14 million cases powers continuous innovations in aligner materials, software algorithms, and 3D force systems helping the Invisalign® system to be used as a premier choice to treat a wide range of cases, from teens to adults.

https://AlignTech.com

Alpha Bio Tec

Alpha Bio Tec has mastered the art of simplifying implant technology by developing implants based on two connections - an internal hex connection and a conical hex connection. They innovated the creation of a "one-platform-fits-all" prosthetic system which allows dentists to use a single restoration line for each implant platform. Additionally, all their implants, abutments, and surgical tools take existing systems into account in order to simplify work and minimize customer learning curves. Consequently, their surgical kit is compatible with all products and includes everything from basic surgical instrumentation to advanced therapy tools. These advancements in addition to simplifying work processes have led their products to have an impressive overall implant clinical success rate of 99.6%.

https://Alpha-Bio.net

American Dental Institute

Located in Orlando, FL, The American Dental Institute (ADI) brings together top trainers from around the world into a single International Hub to offer a collaborative relationship-driven dental training solution to create a VIP CE experience. They are dedicated to elevating dentistry with the highest quality international dental influencers from around the globe to collaborate and build a lasting community. Envisioned by dentists and for dentists, American Dental Institute was born with the mission of offering the best quality of training programs in Dentistry, taught by world-class faculty in a state-of-the-art facility. ADI teaches dental professionals worldwide to stay competitive and ahead of the curve through quality lectures and hands-on programs internationally certified, allowing you to improve your skills and practice.

https://AmericanDentalInstitute.com

A. Titan Instruments

Family founded and operated since 1998, A. Titan is built on a solid foundation of three principles: quality, trust, and tradition. It's A. Titan's mission to enhance the quality of patient care by providing superior products and instrumentation on the cutting edge of dentistry. Located in Orchard Park, NY their world class manufacturing facility and corporate office spans 110,000 sq. feet. Their engineering team is committed to producing instruments constructed from the highest quality materials that elevate the level of patient care in practices across the world. Maintaining high levels of customer relationship management and working closely with key opinion leaders to provide efficient instrument solutions, A. Titan strives to be your trusted instrument partner.

https://ATitan.com

Australasian Implant Academy

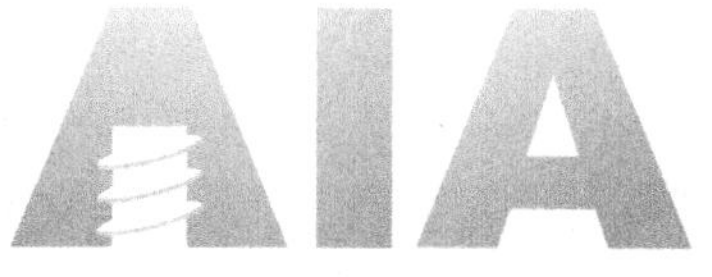

Australasian Implant Academy (AIA) boasts some of the most respected and revered Dentists' including leading implantologist's Dr Dean Licenblat and Dr Ned Restom. The AIA offers a complete implant placement curriculum from basic implantology all the way through to full arch immediate load solutions. This includes Oral Implantology, single, multiple and full arch treatments, periodontics, and soft tissue management as well as comprehensive hands on and training components related to implant prosthesis and final restorative considerations. The AIA has compiled a unique program offering students three fellowship programs that will culminate into a Full Fellowship and is also supplemented by four, live patient surgical externship programs including, basic and intermediate implant placement, advanced grafting program including sinus and block grafts, PRP and PRF, and Full Arch. The curriculum provided by the Institute effectively prepares clinicians for the American Board examination and gives you the confidence to treat a variety of cases with various complexities.

https://AustralasianImplantAcademy.com.au

Benco Dental

Benco Dental is a full-service dental distributor, continually working to simplify dentistry's needs. They offer a variety of supplies and equipment through a national network of over 60 locations and showrooms. As a family-owned enterprise, Benco Dental prides themselves on having the luxury of thinking in decades, not quarters. Their long-term focus has enabled them to become America's most innovative dental distributor, with every innovation designed for a world-class customer service.

https://Benco.com

Biolase

BIOLASE
Advancing Dentistry

BIOLASE, Inc. is a global market leader in the manufacturing and marketing of proprietary dental laser systems. With over 43,300 laser systems sold to date in over 80 countries around the world, BIOLASE lasers are designed to provide clinically superior, patient-friendly results compared to those achieved with traditional instruments. Their mission is to restore and repair dental anatomy, alleviate pain, and reduce fear and anxiety related to dentistry in order to improve patient quality of life. They enable you to elevate their standard of dental care and improve patient outcomes through laser technology.

https://Biolase.com

Black Talon Security

Ransomware and data theft can happen easily. Black Talon Security specializes in cybersecurity for dental practices. Practices are being impacted by data breaches, ransomware, and malware attacks that can shut down and compromise networks for several weeks and cost practices hundreds of thousands of dollars. They scan your computers and firewalls to identify vulnerabilities that hackers use to gain access to your network and steal your data. Their artificial intelligence-based software prevents threats by autonomously responding thus replacing your outdated traditional anti-virus software. They also train your employees, so they don't fall victim to social engineering scams and give up access to your network and data.

https://BlackTalonSecurity.com

Bloomfield CFO

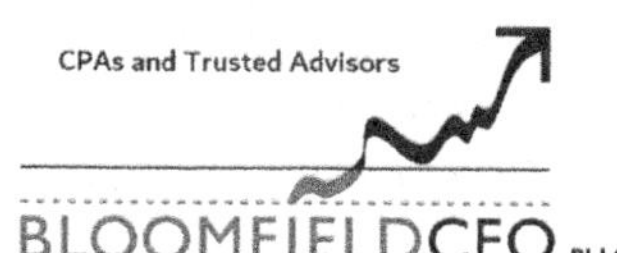

Bloomfield CFO is a boutique advisory firm specializing in financial accounting, taxes and estate planning for dentists nationwide.

They take a proactive role in addressing your practice challenges and opportunities, including practice analytics and management advisory services. In addition, they offer a full range of Fractional CFO Services:

- Short-term and long-term planning for business and personal budgets
- Coaching to ensure proper safeguards and financial foundations are in place
- Practice growth and capital management
- Strategic analysis and financial services
- Tax compliance and planning services
- Merger and acquisition advisory services

At Bloomfield CFO, they only have one agenda – Yours.

https://BloomfieldCFO.com

Burkhart Dental

Burkhart Dental provides quality dental supplies, equipment and technology with full-service at a fair price. Since 1888 Burkhart has been providing win-win solutions for their clients, freeing you up to do what you and your team do best: working with patients, donating your time, learning as much as you can about the business of dentistry, and pushing the industry forward through innovative thinking. Their associates are continuously investing in their training to ensure you have access to necessary knowledge on everything from clinical to business practices. Coming up with new ways to help improve efficiencies, leverage advanced technologies, and reduce your overhead costs – all while maximizing your practice's revenue opportunities.

https://BurkhartDental.com

CareCredit

CareCredit helps you keep more patients smiling with their flexible financing options. This healthcare credit card has been helping patients access needed care for more than 30 years and currently has more than 8.5 million cardholders. CareCredit helps empower your patients to focus on dental needs, while keeping their financial health in mind. When you offer CareCredit, you're helping your patients fit dental care into their budgets with a flexible payment option. In turn, this can help them accept and follow through on the treatment that they want and need. CareCredit offers training, scripting, POS materials, and more, to help ensure that payment conversations are as easy as possible and as friendly as the smiles you serve. And when you join the CareCredit dental community, there are specialists across their network - from general dentists to endodontists and orthodontists - who can provide helpful industry insights and assist your patients in getting the care they want and need today.

https://CareCredit.com

CEDR HR Solutions

HR issues are a constant challenge for practice owners. Having an up-to-date employee handbook that is compliant with all federal, state, county and city laws is important for you and your employees helps you save time and reduce liability. CEDR HR Solutions provides free streamlined HR software, so you stay compliant and manage employee agreements, track work hours and PTO, and provide your new hires with important HIPAA training.

https://CEDRSolutions.com

Champion Dentists

The Champion Dentists program helps you operate your dental practice at the highest level of performance and profitability. Those lucky enough to be chosen for this elite performance-based coaching and consulting program learn to elevate all aspects of operating your dental business. Whether your goal is to increase new patient attraction, boost your case acceptance, or optimize your staff retention and loyalty, this program has been designed to maximize the valuation of your dental business.

This productivity program uses a proprietary, process-driven, systematic approach to identify, evaluate and address key opportunities that drive your results. They use an advanced methodology that helps you generate lasting results increasing both your gross revenue and net profit quickly and consistently. Plus, Champion Dentist partners learn a proven leadership process to build a "Championship Culture" that elevates your staff productivity, happiness and loyalty. Best of all, this win-win program is delivered through a no-risk partnership agreement where you only pay after you experience results, and your revenue rises. Schedule your complimentary profit optimization assessment call today to see how much additional revenue your practice is capable of.

https://ChampionDentists.com

ClearChoice

Since 2005, ClearChoice Dental Implant Centers have helped restore hope and confidence in more than 145,000 patients across the United States through advanced oral treatments that can lead to better overall health and quality of life. Equipped with innovative technology, including 3D CBCT Scan technology and a full-service, on-site lab, each ClearChoice Dental Implant Center is owned and operated by a licensed and experienced dental expert, providing comprehensive dental implant treatment services in advanced, all-in-one treatment facilities. ClearChoice performs the entire dental implant process all under one roof, for one price, including any extractions needed, the surgery, and the placement of the implants. A multidisciplinary team of doctors continues to work with patients throughout the healing process to refine their smiles, make any changes they want to the color, size, and fit of the teeth. Dental implants offer a solution that is the closest thing to natural teeth, and with proper care and maintenance, can last 25 years.

https://ClearChoice.com

Colgate

Colgate makes toothpaste, toothbrushes and mouthwash products that promote healthy smiles. Not only because having a healthy smile is important to your overall health, but because when you have a healthy smile, you actually smile more – and that's a powerful thing. People trust Colgate products to freshen breath, enhance cavity and plaque prevention, enamel protection, tartar control, and improve tooth whitening.

https://Colgate.com

Crest + Oral B

Crest has been a leader in dental health innovations since its inception in 1955. Crest was a pioneer in stannous fluoride toothpaste and has since evolved their product line to include Oral-B toothbrushes, advanced mouthwash products and teeth whitening treatments. Crest is on a mission to close America's smile gap and improve the dental care habits of children everywhere with a commitment of providing oral care to 20 million children in need by 2030.

https://Crest.com

Curve Dental

Founded in 2004, Curve Dental's goal is to deliver cloud-based software that makes it easy to manage your dental practice. From scheduling, billing, texting, patient engagement, imaging, charting, reports/dashboards, implementation, support, training, and data conversion, Curve Dental seeks to deliver the industry's best all-in-one practice management solution for independent practices and multisite/DSOs. Serving over 50,000 dental professionals within the United States and Canada, the company is singularly focused on the dental industry and is committed to delivering the best all-in-one dental practice management and patient engagement software for practices of all sizes.

https://CurveDental.com

Darby Dental

Darby is one of the nation's largest providers of dental supplies and solutions, offering more than 50,000 products and an extensive range of capital equipment, software, technology, and repair services. Widely recognized for excellence in customer service, highly competitive prices, and innovative value-added solutions, Darby works with practices of all sizes, as well as a number of specialties, and government institutions.

https://DarbyDental.com

DDS Match

DDS Match specializes in connecting dental practice buyers and sellers by integrating tremendous relationship capabilities, using a unique process for dentists, "The Trusted Transition Process," supported by a robust website and professional advice. Thad Miller, founder of DDSmatch.com, envisioned a better way for dentists to make dental practice transitions by pairing technology with a human touch to produce a professional and exacting match. Their advisors serve their clients through practice sales, mergers, dental partnership agreements, associate placements, dental office appraisals and dental real estate sales.

https://DDSMatch.com

Dedicated Implants

Dedicated Implants is a multi-specialty medical group that provides Dentist, Oral Surgeon, and Physician support services including health plan contracts, comprehensive proprietary software, and total claims management for full-arch implant cases. Simply put, they help dentists receive considerably higher and more consistent in-network reimbursements through their patients Blue Cross Blue Shield (BCBS) medical insurance. They've cracked the code allowing patients with BCBS to use their insurance card instead of their credit card to get the surgery they need without having to mortgage their homes to do so.

Dedicated Implants can help you close more consults, perform more surgeries, make more money, and help more patients receive the life-changing implants they so desperately need but might not be able to afford otherwise. Stop turning away 60-70% of patients simply because they can't afford treatment. Let Dedicated Implants in-network medical reimbursement system help you convert more of those initial consults into some of your most profitable cases.

https://ImplantCoverage.com

Delta Dental

Delta Dental is the nation's leading provider of dental insurance. Delta Dental serves more than 80 million Americans, protecting more smiles than any other dental benefits company, with the largest network of dentists nationwide, they provide quick answers and personalized service. Their core purpose is the advancement of the oral health of their customers, partners and consumers through dental insurance and the philanthropic efforts of Delta Dental companies. Through their national network of Delta Dental companies, they offer dental coverage in all 50 states, Washington, D.C. and Puerto Rico, with a local presence in communities across the country, providing groups and individuals with quality, cost-effective dental insurance and superior customer service.

https://DeltaDental.com

Dental Compliance Specialists

Dental Compliance Specialists (DCS) is run by Duane Tinker, a former Texas state police investigator for the Texas Dental Board who traded his badge and gun for the opportunity to help dentists protect themselves, their patients, and their practices when it comes to legal compliance. DCS works with dentists on concerns involving HIPAA compliance, dental board rules (including sedation requirements, infection control, business promotion, recordkeeping, standard of care, licensing requirements); DEA regulations; standards of emergency medical care; Medicaid requirements; infection control (including CDC guidelines, dental board rules, AAMI/ANSI standards); ADA/AAOMS/AAPD guidelines; CDT/CPT/HCPC/ICD-10 Codes; and OIG compliance program guidance. Protect your practice by contacting Dental Compliance Specialists today.

https://DentalCompliance.com

Dental Cooperative

Dental Cooperative is the oldest and largest cooperative of independent dentists in the nation. As the antithesis of corporate dentistry, they exclusively serve the independent dentist community. Members are practicing independent dentists working collectively for better solutions. They are dedicated to providing real solutions for the issues facing independent dentists today and in the future.

https://DentalCooperative.com

Dental Menu

dental menu

Does your practice offer dental subscription plans to your patients? If not, Dental Menu can help you add this predictable revenue stream to your practice. Providing this alternative to dental insurance for the uninsured unlocks new growth opportunities for your business while providing care for those who deserve it. Dental Menu gives you a complete platform to offer subscription plans directly to your patients giving them a menu of services to choose from. This gives you a predictable revenue stream while empowering your patients to design an affordable dental care plan to fit their budget and needs.

https://DentalMenu.com

Dental Hearts

Dental Hearts is a charity that provides low-cost and no-cost implants to U.S. Military Veterans, homeless and low-income seniors. Started by Dr. Joe Mehranfar and Scott Lauer with a mission of helping the 400,000+ Arizona veterans and the majority of the population that would benefit from dental implants but cannot afford conventional private practice fees, the organization runs a world-class dental implant facility in Phoenix, AZ restoring confidence, allowing people to eat most of the foods they enjoy, and allowing them to smile again.

https://DentalHearts.org

Dental Intelligence

Dental Intelligence software helps dental professionals intelligently shape the future of your practice so you can focus on your patients without getting caught in the weeds. Their software solution streamlines office efficiency with systems that make sense quickly and easily. It helps you reduce wait times, customize treatment plans on the fly, and easily present detailed payment plans and financing options. Your staff can automatically schedule future appointments, seamlessly collect payment balances, get more reviews from happy patients, and add your personal touch to follow-ups without hours of housekeeping work.

https://DentalIntel.com

Dental Robot

Dental Robot is an integrated intelligent automation AI tool that helps you save hundreds of hours per week executing repetitive tasks. Regardless of your processes and workflows or the type of software and web applications that you use, Dental Robot adapts to your office. From automating Google reviews, insurance reimbursement, teledentistry, insurance verification, or financial accounting, Dental Robot helps you reduce staff time spent on repetitive manual tasks that can be completed by their advanced AI.

https://DentalRobot.ai

Dental Warranty

Dental Warranty provides a unique protection plan on dental treatment and appliances. Their promise is to help you maintain the restorative, cosmetic, and removable dentistry you deliver in good condition and working order. From fillings to implants to sleep apnea appliances, Dental Warranty offers you a unique practice growth opportunity. While providing your patients peace-of-mind knowing they are protected against dog-chewed dentures, sports injuries, new decay, and whatever else might threaten their new smile. Patients can redeem their coverage with any dentist nationwide if they aren't able to make it back to the original performing dentist for care.

https://DentalWarrantyCorp.com

Dental Whale

DentalWhale

Dental Whale provides dental professionals with a suite of practical, efficient practice management solutions under one digital roof. In addition to the 4th largest fleet of dental technicians in the nation and an exclusive online education platform, they offer heavily discounted members-only savings on thousands of items in their online supplies store. From latex gloves to 3D scanners, their members enjoy up to 40% savings on supplies, labs and equipment.

https://DentalWhale.com

Dentrix

Dentrix is a leading practice management software designed to enhance the dental office experience. Dentrix is an integrated technology platform designed to boost the productivity and efficiency of your practice. From business management data analytics to automated data backups, electronic claims, payment card processing, automated billing statements, website development tools, appointment reminders, and voice recognition software, Dentrix can help you improve staff productivity, expand your clinical efficiencies and streamline your office workflow.

https://Dentrix.com

Dexis

Dexis solutions brings you the industry's most comprehensive selection of diagnostic imaging products, intelligently designed to deliver a complete workflow. The award-winning DTX Studio Clinic puts you and your patients at the center, simplifying the interaction with your patient scans and images, and making each appointment more focused and valuable for everyone. From image acquisition to diagnostics and treatment planning, DTX Studio Clinic brings all of your X-rays, photos, 2D and 3D, extraoral and intraoral imaging formats into one clear, comprehensive view. Dexis offers leading products for X-ray generation, intraoral digital radiography, intraoral scanning, panoramic and cephalometric imaging, 3D CBCT imaging, and treatment planning software so you'll have everything you need for efficient, effective, and accurate diagnosis and treatment planning through one reliable and experienced partner.

https://Dexis.com

Digital Dentistry Institute

The Digital Dentistry Institute provides instruction to members of the dental profession that is consistent with the highest standards of treatment and the highest levels of clinical success determined by both the dentist and the patient. Promoting mentorship as a foundation for learning in the field of advanced comprehensive dentistry, DDI is committed to assisting each doctor, following their training, and in the implementation of that training in their practice. DDI provides exceptional education programs globally designed to train and guide you to provide the highest possible quality of care in the field of advanced comprehensive dentistry and related fields using state-of-the-art, technologically relevant, online, and hands-on training for the dentist and dental personnel.

https://DDIDental.com

DoWell Dental Products

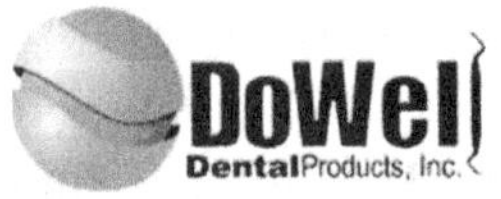

DoWell Dental Products is a premier dental instrument manufacturer. They offer an extensive collection of surgical, operative, diagnostic, hygiene, crown and sinus instruments and equipment to give you advanced solutions to provide quality care. DoWell Dental Products thrives on the leading edge of innovative products, excellent customer service, and giving back to the community.

https://DoWellDentalProducts.com

Envista

Envista is a global family of more than 30 trusted dental brands operating in over 120 countries all united by a shared purpose: to partner with professionals to improve lives. Envista helps its partners deliver the best possible patient care through industry-leading products, solutions, and technology. From digital consultation and modeling tools to superior equipment and surgical instruments, Envista companies support dental professionals at every patient interaction, with increasingly integrated digital workflows.

Their Specialty Products and Technology division develops a wide variety of leading brands including Nobel Biocare, Ormco, Spark Clear Aligner System, Implant Direct, Orascoptic and AlphaBio. In addition, Envista manufactures leading equipment and consumables including Dexis, Kerr, Metrex and DTX Studio.

https://EnvistaCo.com

Henry Schein

Henry Schein is a world-class solutions company for dental professionals powered by a network of people and technology. Powered by over 22,000 team members worldwide, the company's network of trusted advisors provides more than 1 million customers globally with more than 300 valued solutions that help improve operational success and clinical outcomes. Their business, clinical, technology, and supply chain solutions help office-based dental practitioners work more efficiently so you can provide quality care more effectively. Beyond supplies, the company provides equipment, repairs, practice management software, and digital technology.

https://HenrySchein.com

HOA.com

HOA.com is a community engagement platform that connects homeowners to professionals they can trust. Targeting the 370,000+ neighborhoods and communities managed by homeowner associations, their hyper-local social farming system helps you become the recognized and respected dentist to homeowners in the local neighborhoods nearest to your practice. Homeowners are likely the perfect prospects for your practice as they have higher incomes and assets and can afford more costly dental procedures. HOA.com's database feed includes over 260 million U.S. consumers including nearly every homeowner in America. Plus, their referral network helps you build referral partnerships with local business owners and professionals who serve homeowners every day and are looking for quality dentists they can refer their clients to.

https://HOA.com/dental

Hu-FriedyGroup

HuFriedyGroup
a STERIS company

With over 200 years of collective experience in the dental industry, HuFriedyGroup is a global leader in dental instrument manufacturing, infection prevention, and instrument reprocessing workflows.

HuFriedyGroup helps dental professionals be the best in practice by providing a complete circle of protection in the dental suite, bringing together world-class products, services, education, and communities that result in superior clinician performance, clinical outcomes, and safety for clinicians and patients. Headquartered in Chicago, HuFriedyGroup products are distributed in more than 100 countries, and the dental division maintains offices in Germany, Italy, China, and Japan.

https://HuFriedyGroup.com

Implant Direct

Implant Direct was founded in 2006 with the bold concept of making high-quality implants accessible to clinicians and the patients you serve. All implants are made in California and manufactured under rigorous FDA standards. Their practical innovation approach focuses on usability, pragmatism and simplicity. They offer easy ordering online or by phone and have localized sales and clinical support teams to optimize your results. From immediate placement to full arch, Implant Direct offers guided workflow to help you navigate surgery with confidence and excellence.

https://ImplantDirect.com

Implant Education Center

Implant Education Company offers dental implant training delivered in a world-class facility in sunny Phoenix AZ. They offer dental implant CE courses focused on implant dentistry as a whole, All-on-4® and sinus lift procedures to a variety of dentists, from those starting out their journey to dentists looking to advance their skill set to offer patients more advanced cases. Their courses are focused more on quality than quantity with the goal for you to learn and understand the principles and fundamentals of implant dentistry to ensure successful treatments. After you experience their didactic training, you will treat live patients under the guidance of our expert instructors in small student to teacher ratios with two instructors to six attending dentists ensuring you get the direction and coaching that you need to be successful in implant dentistry.

https://implantEdCo.com

InfluentialDentists.com

InfluentialDentists.com helps high-achieving dentists and CEOs to leverage their influence so they can change the face of the planet. Influential Dentists have certain key strategies in common. They have clarity on what matters personally, they set goals with a valid mission and vision, they plan, collaborate and form strategic relationships, they have a coach and accountability, they execute, and they celebrate successes. Leveraging influence can single handedly help you to buy back your time, grow your practice(s) and begin enjoying a better quality of life.

There are many ways to elevate your influence. It is sustainable and creates wealth and a legacy. InfluentialDentists.com offers professional coaching and consulting, and a mastermind for dentists who are looking to take influence to the next level.

https://InfluentialDentists.com

Intelibly

Intelibly is a robust data platform that connects patients to trusted providers through multiple sources. Consider registering your practice on Intelibly.com and list your services through their FinderConnect system which includes a built-in Book Now button that can easily be added to your existing website. They also offer a ScheduleConnect API that allows you to improve your online scheduling and patient communication. Lastly, their Comply 133 tool makes compliance easy enabling you to accurately demonstrate a pattern of compliance to the HR 133 provider directory mandate.

https://Intelibly.com

JK Dental Group

JK Dental Group

Perhaps best known for their BiLumix Surgical Headlamp and award-winning Rayscan CBCT, JK Dental Group provides innovative, cutting-edge digital imaging solutions and dental equipment. Their CAS-200 Silence machine is an industry-leading extra-oral chair-side aerosol suction machine that eliminates aerosols and up to 99.9995% of all airborne particulates and pathogens, decreasing the potential spread of infections and disease.

https://JKDentalGroup.com

Kerr

For over 125 years, Kerr has been serving the comprehensive needs of the entire dental care community in pursuit of enhancing oral health. Individual Kerr brands are encompassed within the Kerr Restoratives, Kerr Endodontics, Kerr Rotary, and Kerr TotalCare product lines. Kerr designs and manufactures products for all aspects of modern restorative dentistry. Their knowledgeable field service works closely with a network of exclusive stockists to provide technical training and support to strengthen their position as a world market leader. They offer advanced aesthetic dentistry through education and sustainable solutions based on ideas from the real world, making the Kerr name synonymous with integrity among dentists worldwide.

https://KerrDental.com

Mango Voice

Mango Voice is a VOIP phone system that is perfect for helping you streamline your dental practice operation. Powerful features like click to call and multiple phone lines help your front office team work more efficiently and effectively. You can even route calls to your cell phone to support your patients from anywhere. When a known number calls in, Mango Voice displays the patient's name and any upcoming appointment info on your computer screen. This allows your team to instantly tailor the conversation to each patient's unique needs, remind them of their upcoming appointments, and easily reschedule if needed. This quality customer service increases patient loyalty while saving time for your staff. Mango Voice provides essential features for the modern world, including routing your office phone to your cell, converting voicemails to email so you can quickly review the content of a message, and SMS auto replies.

https://MangoVoice.com

Masters Arch

Master's Arch is a dental laboratory that specializes in full-arch and dental cosmetic treatments, committed to raising the bar in the dental industry and making sure no edentulous people are left behind. Their comprehensive services are designed to provide the best quality dental restoration solutions for patients, utilizing the latest technology and materials available. They value teamwork (including a restorative doctor, surgeon, lab, and sales rep) in their workflow, and prioritize communication with their clients. Sean Han, CDT serves as CEO and Co-Founder of Master's Arch and is a respected global expert to various premier dental implant manufacturers, dental CAD software companies, and high-end material manufacturers. He continues to research and develop both prosthetic and treatment workflow solutions for full arch and cosmetic dental treatments working with dental providers nationwide.

https://MAProviders.com

MCS Infection Control Solutions

Providing your patients with a sterile facility is what they expect and deserve, but how do you know if your facility is clean? Unfortunately, most dental offices are filled with invisible viruses and germs. That's why MCS Infection Control Solutions provides a proprietary 6-step electrostatic cleaning process to spray all surfaces with their patented solution that is both FDA and EPA approved. This anti-viral solution protects against microbial activity for up to three months giving you a competitive advantage and your patients peace of mind.

https://MCSteams.com

Nexhealth

NexHealth provides practices with an all-in-one patient experience platform featuring online booking, integrated forms, patient reviews, payments, and more. Today, over 6,000 practices across North America choose NexHealth as their patient experience platform because it's the only solution that syncs in real-time with dozens of health record systems. On average, practices see 18 more patients a month and save 3+ hours a day with NexHealth's platform."

https://MCSteams.com

Metrex Infection Prevention

Metrex
INFECTION PREVENTION

Since 1985 Metrex has supported healthcare professionals dedicated to eliminating Healthcare associated infections. They offer a system of solutions designed to address cross-contamination across your entire healthcare facility including quality infection prevention solutions that help increase compliance, improve back-office efficiencies and enhance quality patient care. Their complete line of infection control products includes surface disinfectants, hand hygiene products, barriers, and bib holders.

https://Metrex.com

Nobel Biocare

Nobel Biocare is a leading innovator of implant-based dental restorations, an industry the company pioneered thanks to PerIngvar Brånemark's ground-breaking discovery of osseointegration in 1952. Since then, they've helped treat millions of patients with their science-backed and forward-looking solutions. Nobel Biocare supports its customers through all phases of professional development, offering world-class training and education along with practice support and patient information materials. The company is headquartered in Zurich, Switzerland with production facilities at four sites located in the United States, Sweden and Japan. Products and services are available in over 80 countries through subsidiaries and distributors. The company's portfolio offers solutions from single tooth to fully edentulous indications with dental implant systems (including key brands NobelActive and NobelParallel and ceramic implant NobelPearl*), a comprehensive range of high-precision individualized prosthetics, and CAD/CAM systems (NobelProcera), digital solutions for treatment planning and guided surgery (NobelClinician and DTX Studio suite) as well as biomaterials.

https://NobelBiocare.com

Novadontics

Novadontics® is the world's first cloud-based practice management software for general and implant practices of any size. Novadontics helps clinicians provide the highest level of patient care with innovative, integrated features and industry-leading tools with mobile access from any web-enabled device, allowing clinicians and staff to run their practices smoothly and efficiently while keeping their focus on their patients. Novadontics is leading the way with tremendous discounts on high-quality products, its network of experts providing online and on-site consultation support, and its second-to-none continuing education platform. This all-in-one solution includes everything dentists need to efficiently manage your practice, optimize patient care, and grow your business.

https://Novadontics.com

OneClickReferral

OneClick Referral is an innovative tool that connects dental colleagues like never before, to easily communicate and refer patients to one another. OneClick Referral is simple to install, with seamless integration with your current dental practice management system. This web-based software integrates with Dentrix, Eaglesoft, OpenDental among others and is built for general dentists to immediately send referrals to oral surgeons, periodontists, endodontists, prosthodontists, orthodontists and dental labs. Imagine having more time to do what you do best: take care of patients and yourself.

https://OneClickReferral.com

Open Dental

Open Dental is an open-source dental practice management software that is comprehensive and highly customizable. This solution offers dental practice management software at an affordable price for practices of any size. The software supports all aspects of your practice including appointment scheduling, treatment planning, charting, imaging, eServices, accounting, HR and referral tracking.

https://OpenDental.com

Oragen

Oragen is a doctor-centric organization that helps oral surgeons start, sell, and/or transition their practices. Funded by a family office, Oragen ensures that its oral surgeons are cared for and provided the resources they need to successfully navigate the new world of consolidation. Combining oral surgery practice acquisition and de novo buildouts with substantial organizational resources and capital, Oragen helps surgeons take their practices to the next level.

https://Oragen.com

Orascoptic

Orascoptic provides a superior line of dental loupes to ensure you can perform your procedures with exactness. As a dental professional, your work is on display in every smile that walks out of your practice. Dentistry requires exceptional visualization, unique skills, and precision which can leave you vulnerable to unnatural body positioning for long periods of time. Orascoptic's custom-fit loupes and headlights enable you to work with superior visualization to see the unseen, and practice pain-free. During an in-office consultation, their experts will guide you to the right custom-crafted loupe and headlight for your practice.

https://Orascoptic.com

Ormco

Ormco has nearly 60 years of distinguished history in providing the orthodontic profession with a breadth of high quality, innovative products and solutions backed by attentive customer service and educational support. The company manufactures quality aligners, archwires, auxiliaries, brackets, tubes, bands, and self-ligation products to help you deliver minimally invasive treatment protocols that provide remarkable advantages for you and your patients.

https://Ormco.com

Pearl AI

Pearl is the first real-time dental artificial intelligence platform that automatically detects numerous conditions in dental x-rays to give dentists a second set of eyes for superior radiologic accuracy. Spin your practice data into more profit, higher practitioner performance and better patient health with computer vision-enabled clinical performance insights. Pearl was founded on the notion that artificial intelligence can be the dental practitioner's always-on assistant and the patient's most trustworthy friend. Its founders have a uniquely personal connection to the dental industry's intricacies, as well as the knowledge and education to actualize the full and practicable potential that AI has to offer. They are applying their passion and decades of combined experience in technology entrepreneurship, dental healthcare, and medical imaging AI to establish a new, higher standard of care in dentistry.

https://HelloPearl.com

Pearson Dental Supplies

Pearson Dental Supply has supplied generations of dentists with high-quality dental supplies and equipment they need on a daily basis. As an authorized dealer of high-quality national brands, Pearson Dental Supply hosts a large inventory of authentic FDA-approved products that are backed by warranties and liability insurance. With 10 branches across the United States and more than 130,000 products in stock, Pearson Dental Supply can offer all the benefits of a large supply dealer without the red tape and hassle you commonly find with corporations.

https://PearsonDental.com

Proceed Finance

Proceed Finance are patient financing experts providing your patients simple and affordable payment options for the treatments you provide. The Proceed Finance model is simple – fully-funded, fast delivery financing for providers and easy to understand terms and the lowest rates for patients. With online applications requiring limited information, your patients will get instant decisions in most cases so they can say YES to more procedures with a great financing option you can trust.

https://ProceedFinance.com

Restored Smiles Implant Training

RS RESTORED SMILES. IMPLANT TRAINING WITH A PURPOSE

If you are looking for implant training, the Restored Smiles Ranch experience is like no other in dentistry. With a destination that is set in a peaceful countryside setting surrounded by Santa Barbara County ranches, The RS experience provides a unique setting for learning, creativity, relaxation and retention. When the mind is allowed to learn in a stress-free environment, research has shown that all senses can be engaged to help more easily and accurately absorb what is being taught. In addition, the RS dental learning experience is designed to enhance the bonds built within the community. The opportunity for doctors to be themselves in a safe environment for interactive learning further enhances the enrichment attendees receive during each course, taught by highly credentialed and experienced trainers.

https://restoredsmilescourses.com/rs-ranch-experience

RingCentral

RingCentral

RingCentral is the world's leading cloud phone system that puts connection at the center of your care. Build lasting patient relationships by improving communication before, during and after treatment. RingCentral helps you improve patient experiences while reducing costs with modern and secure cloud communications.

https://RingCentral.com

Seattle Study Club

SEATTLE STUDY CLUB®
Cultivating Excellence in Comprehensive Dentistry

Seattle Study Club is an international network of dental professionals interested in furthering their knowledge and providing excellent care. There are more than 250 dental study clubs in their network located all over the world. Each study club meets regularly for interactive educational programs, discussion on the latest developments in dentistry, and presentations by world-renowned clinical speakers. These meetings provide a forum for each member doctor to discuss and plan cases by drawing on the collective knowledge of the entire group.

https://SeattleStudyClub.com

Smile Source

Smile Source
PRIVATE PRACTICE NETWORK

Smile Source is a family of over 1,000 dentists & 625 private dental practices working together to provide world-class patient care. They operate through a "doctors helping doctors" model to band together private practices who enjoy the same buying power and collaboration that bigger companies benefit from. SmileSource dentists collectively buy over $85 million in products & services each year ensuring engaged members receive back more than the cost of their membership.

https://SmileSource.com

Spark Clear Aligner System

Trusted by orthodontists worldwide, Spark is a nearly invisible aligner said to be more comfortable and to stain less than the leading aligner brand. Spark Aligners are made with TruGEN™, the latest innovation in clear aligner material. Manufactured with polished and scalloped edges, Spark Aligners are designed to provide a more comfortable treatment experience while supporting more efficient and effective tooth movement. Spark Aligners are BPA, mercury, latex, and phthalate-free and can treat a variety of teeth-straightening cases, including crowding, spacing, open bite, underbite, overbite, and crossbite.

https://SparkAligners.com

Speaking Consulting Network

Since 1997, the Speaking Consulting Network (SCN) has been helping dentists transform their experience into a profitable speaking and consulting career. Whether you're a current or aspiring author, podcaster, social media influencer or international dental speaker, this community helps launch your dental speaking and consulting career so you get booked and paid. Led by international speaker and author Ryan Vet, SCN gives you access to an online vault of training tools, videos, webinars and resources to elevate your credibility and visibility.

https://SpeakingConsultingNetwork.com

UltraDent

Ultradent sells a full line of dental and orthodontics products in over 130 countries through its international network of distributors, dealers, and direct sales locations. For over 40 years, Ultradent has been on a mission to improve oral health globally through science, creativity, and education. They strive to provide clinicians with progressive and trustworthy solutions while always respecting the patient and promoting their well-being.

https://Ultradent.com

Van Hook Dental Lab

Van Hook Dental Studio is a full-service, national dental laboratory who knows that changing a smile changes a life. They understand that your patients have high expectations and are happy to help you exceed them. Through digital technology, their talented ceramists create the finest cosmetic crowns, bridges, and veneers using high quality materials to craft natural-looking restorations. They also produce superior dentures, implants, aligners, and nightguards working in accordance with your preferences to deliver precise and esthetic results.

https://VHDental.com

VYNE Dental

Vyne Dental improves your billing cycle, so you get paid faster making it easier for patients to pay via text or email. They develop solutions for dental practices and insurance plans and payers that facilitate the secure exchange of health information in a digital, end-to-end revenue cycle that optimizes your cash flow while reducing associative costs. You're delivering quality care in a timely manner and should be getting reimbursed for that care in a similarly timely fashion. Vyne's solution simplifies the claims processing, attachments, and secure messaging that is essential for your practice to run smoothly.

https://VyneDental.com

W&H Dental

W&H Dental manufactures precision instruments and high-end restoration, prosthetics, prophylaxis, periodontology, endodontics, oral surgery, and sterilization products and solutions. Developed and produced at sites in Austria, Italy and Sweden, the company supports dentists in over 130 countries including the USA, Europe and Asia.

https://WH.com

Weave

Weave is a telephony solution that brings together a world-class phone system and a suite of communication tools, so it's easy to automate more tasks, keep schedules full, get paid faster, collect more reviews and much more. Weave consolidates everything you need to keep in touch with your patients into one easy-to-use piece of software. Get more reviews, fuller schedules, faster payments and more patient loyalty with greater customer efficiency - all in one unified platform.

https://GetWeave.com

WEO Media

WEO Media is an award-winning, full-service dental marketing agency serving hundreds of general dental and specialty practices nationwide. Doctors frequently chose WEO Media to be their trusted marketing partner due to an excellent return on investment (ROI), outstanding customer service, highly effective marketing programs, and deep dental industry knowledge. WEO Media has won the Cellerant Technology "Best of Class" Award four times for being the best website and online marketing company in the dental industry. This is the top award in the dental industry and is presented every year at the annual ADA conference. WEO Media's comprehensive dental marketing services include secure, fully responsive websites, search engine optimization (SEO), pay-per-click (PPC) campaigns, online reputation management, social media management, patient education website videos, custom video production, 24/7 live chat, direct mail campaigns, patient newsletters, secure online patient forms, photography, graphic design, branding, Premium Healthgrades profiles, and more. WEO Media has been a Google Certified Partner Agency for nearly a decade, and a Healthgrades Partner Agency for almost as long. The company was founded in 2009, and is based in Portland, Oregon.

https://WeoMedia.com

X-Nav Technologies

X-Nav Technologies is a medical device company that develops surgical products for the dental market. Their X-Guide Dynamic 3D Navigation system supports more accurate implant surgery allowing you to control the exact placement of implant position, angle and depth during live surgery. Interactive, turn-by-turn guidance gives you the ability to improve every movement of your handpiece during osteotomy and implant delivery for more exact implant placement - like GPS for your drill. With over 350+ cumulative years of medical/dental product experience, their team consists of advanced optical CT guidance scientists, dental/medical planning software experts, leading dental CBCT engineers, and clinical and industry relation experts. Developed in close collaboration with leading oral and maxillofacial surgeons, the X-Guide system promises to deliver what today's implant clinicians are looking for.

https://X-NavTech.com

Yapi

yapi

Yapi is dental software that syncs seamlessly to your PMS to help you fill your schedule by automating online patient booking through appointment reminders and recall. Yapi includes a complimentary online portal for remote access and offers dental phone integration with Mango Voice and RingCentral. Stop wasting valuable time on endless data entry, printing, scanning and shredding paper. From new patient online forms, electronic treatment plans to automated appointment reminders and online scheduling, Yapi allows your patients to fill out and sign patient forms via an iPad anywhere in your office or through your practice's website from the convenience of their home computer or mobile device.

https://YapiApp.com

Young Dental

YOUNG®

Since 1900, Young Dental has been focused on developing preventive dentistry products. Producing over 100 million disposable prophy angles each year, Young Dental is one of the world's largest manufacturers of disposable prophy angles and preventive dental products.

https://YoungDental.com

ZLinked Marketing

If you're looking to grow your practice and attract new patients, ZLinked Marketing offers a complete and comprehensive "Done-for-You" social media management solution to save you and your team, time, effort and money. Focus on what you do best while we focus on promoting your business through social media. You'll always own it and can add your personal touch directly at any time. ZLinked is flexible, customizable and compliments all web and SEO companies. They create the content for you and include advertising in all of their packages posting to Facebook, Instagram, Twitter, Pinterest, and Google, as well as your personal and business LinkedIn accounts consistently on your behalf.

https://ZLinkedMarketing.com

Zana

zana

If you're looking to create a remarkable experience for your patients, check out Zana's Care Beyond the Chair® program. This ingenious rewards program helps build strong loyalty and boost referrals by providing a wow experience for your best patients and partners. Simply send your VIP patients and referral partners one of Zana's Sonic toothbrushes, customized with your practice logo and the patient's name sent in an impressive Care Beyond the Chair® package. This gives them a memorable gift that keeps your brand in their hand and on their mind each and every day as they brush their teeth. They will automatically receive free brush heads as a reward for referrals and re-care, so both happen more consistently and predictably. With a high ROI, this innovative patient care program will raise retention and drive your word-of-mouth referrals.

https://MyZana.com

Use promo code RavingReferrals23 to receive a 23% discount.

Dental Podcasts

To help you stay apprised and educated on the latest advancements and best practices in dentistry, we have compiled the following list of the dental podcasts we find most informative and beneficial for practice growth. Turn your drive time into your mobile university by tuning into these insightful experts and episodes.

Nano Podcast Alliance

Brought to you by Julieanne O'Connor
and Dr. Mike Czubiak DDS

Ready to launch your dental podcast or take it to the next level? Join Julieanne and the Nano Podcast Alliance and say yes to success. The Nano Podcast Alliance was built by a dentist and podcaster who understands the market, the players, and the potential. It was created to enable dental podcasters to enjoy strength in numbers. By teaming up with other podcasters, advertisers take notice. Once you join the Nano Podcast Alliance, Julieanne and her team can start the process of monetizing your podcast and finding you the perfect sponsors. It's easy and it's free.

https://NanoPodcastAlliance.com/

Voices of Dentistry

Hosted by Dr. Mark Costes, Dr. Justin Moody, Dr. Jason Lipscomb, and Dr. Alan Mead

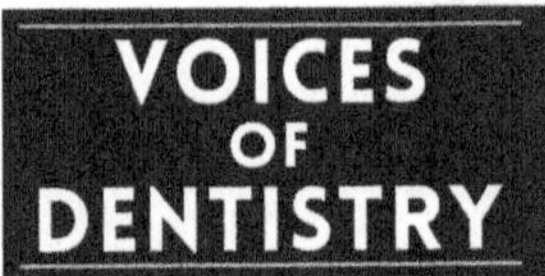

Share your expertise with the dental community through the annual Voices of Dentistry conference. Come meet your favorite dental podcasters, engage with industry-leading speakers, and earn CE credits over one action-packed weekend at the Hilton in Scottsdale, Arizona.

https://VoicesOfDentistry.com/

Advancing Dentistry Podcast

Hosted by Biolase

Top Dental Experts discuss cutting-edge protocols, technologies, and approaches to improving and advancing dental care. Learn how Waterlase laser dentistry improves patient and clinical outcomes straight from successful dentists pioneering new technology.

https://Soundcloud.com/AdvancingDentistryPodcast

Art Of Dental Finance and Management

Hosted by Art Wiederman, CPA

The Art of Dental Finance & Management podcast with Art Wiederman CPA is dedicated to help you meet your personal and business financial goals through tax savings, investing and planning wisely, and managing your dental practice so it can become as profitable as possible.

https://DecisionsInDentistry.com/podcast/

Bulletproof Dental Practice

Hosted by Dr. Peter Boulden & Dr. Craig Spodak

Dentistry is evolving. Is your practice Bulletproof? Join Dr. Peter Boulden & Dr. Craig Spodak to learn proven strategies to grow your practice. Dr. Peter Boulden has an extensive and celebrated list of scholastic achievements in his field, beginning with the very prestigious distinction of Fellow to the Academy of Comprehensive Esthetics (now part of Smile Source network) where he also serves as a member on the Advisory Board.

https://BulletproofDentalPractice.com/category/podcast/

Chew On This

Hosted by Teresa Duncan

As author of *Moving Your Patients to Yes: Easy Insurance Conversations*, and a regular contributing author to the ADA's CDT Companion Guide, Teresa Duncan is a highly sought-after speaker, consultant and coach in the dental industry. After working as a dental assistant, sterilization tech, receptionist and dental office manager, Teresa shares real world experiences to help boost insurance collections and run a more productive and profitable practice.

https://ChewOnThisDentalPodcast.libsyn.com

Delivering WOW

Hosted by Dr. Anissa Holmes

Voted one of the "Top 25 Women in Dentistry" by Dental Products Report, Dr. Anissa Holmes has effectively mastered the skill of the use of social media. With a Facebook following of over 50,000 fans, Dr. Holmes has discovered that the most effective way to get massive results is to first have a vision and to focus on what matters most.

Dr. Holmes teaches you actionable steps to develop your dental practice's culture, systems, and brand as she reveals what works in social media and how to build an amazing dental team. Dr. Holmes shares powerful strategies to help you scale up your business so that you can achieve more while working less.

https://podcasts.apple.com/us/podcast/the-delivering-wow-dental-podcast/id1072610113

Dental Digest

Hosted by Dr. Melissa Seibert

Dental Digest is a dental podcast with a mission of enabling you to stay on the cutting edge of evidence-based dentistry. Dentistry is constantly evolving, but we're here so you can stay up to date while earning CE credits. Topics include operative dentistry, biomimetic dentistry, dental materials, prosthodontics, periodontics, oral surgery, endodontics, orthodontics and more.

https://DentalDigestInstitute.com/

Dental Disrupt

Led by Dr. Jason Lipscomb

Salient

Although not officially a podcast, this list wouldn't be complete if we didn't include Dental Disrupt. Formerly known as Dental Hacks with its legendary podcast run by Dr. Jason Lipscomb, the Dental Disrupt Facebook group is shaking up the industry and turning dentistry on its ear. Here you will learn together with other dental pros, have fun and talk about real things in dentistry.

https://DentalDisrupt.com

Dental Drill Bits

Hosted by Sandy Purdue and Dana Salisbury of Classic Practice Resources

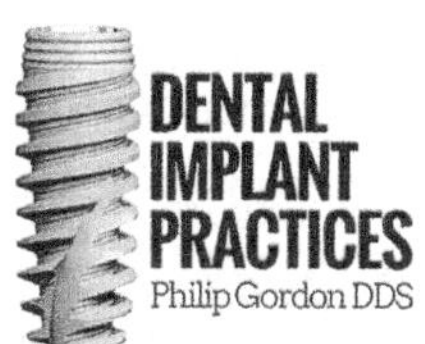

With over 50 years combined experience in the dental industry, Sandy and Dana discuss issues facing the dental practice owner of today. This podcast show features the movers and shakers of the dental industry as well as opinion leaders. Enjoy the fun, laid-back vibe as things get real.

https://podcasts.apple.com/us/podcast/dental-drills-bits/id1193269670

Dental Implant Practices

Hosted by Dr. Philip J. Gordon, DDS

CLASSIC PRACTICE
RESOURCES

Are you looking to incorporate dental implants into your practice or take your implant practice to the next level? This podcast discusses best practices and successful strategies for incorporating dental implants into your practice from a logistical and technical standpoint.

https://www.dentalimplantpractices.com/podcast/

Dental Marketing Mastery

Hosted by William Horrocks

In this podcast, Howie Horrocks and Mark Dilatush share their 30 years of experience in bringing quality new patients to thousands of dental practices across the world.

https://DentalWebcontent.libsyn.com/

Dental Practice Freedom

Hosted by Dr. Steven Schluentz

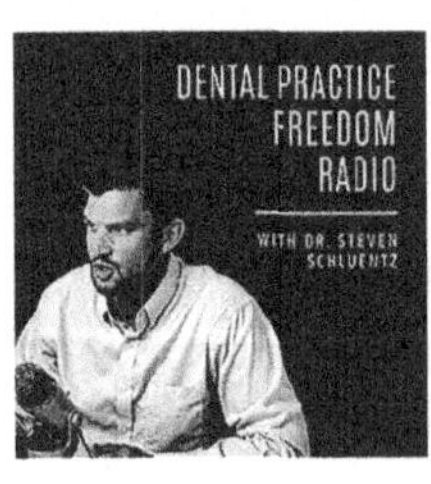

How do Dentists like you, who aren't willing to let insurance companies dictate how you will run your practice, who want to create incredibly profitable practices without sacrificing your time or sanity; how do you create the strategies to ensure your practice not only survives but thrives in the 21st century? That's the blaring question and Dr. Steve Schluentz answers on this intriguing podcast.

https://DentalPracticeFreedomRadio.libsyn.com/

Dental Up Education

Hosted by Shaun Keating of Keating Dental Lab

A great source of insights and dental hacks delivered by dentists and leaders in the industry. Come experience a dentist's best and worst days on the job, find tips and techniques to improve your skills, and learn from the best. We have clinical advice, marketing strategies, office management, technology, hacks and everything in between. Hear about the personal and professional lives of dentists today. With over 200 episodes and counting, they've got all your dental educational and entertainment needs covered!

https://KeatingDentalLab.com/dental-up/

Dentist Money

Hosted by Reese Harper

Join thousands of dentists who are learning how to make smart financial decisions. You'll get straightforward advice about investing, retirement planning, tax reduction, insurance, debt management, and personal finance.

https://ReeseHarper.com/for-dentists/dentist-money-podcast/

Dentistry Made Simple

Hosted by Dr. Tarun "TBone" Agarwal

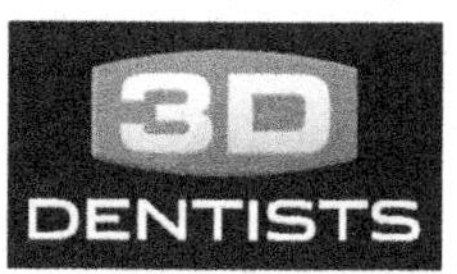

Optimize Your Dental Practice for Revenue Growth & Enjoyment. Dentistry Made Simple podcast gives you an entertaining, yet serious look into the business mindset and clinical skills needed to grow and maintain a thriving dental business. Dr. Tarun

"T-Bone" Agarwal brings years of practical experience and a unique 'in the trenches' view of dentistry to the podcast.

From marketing and branding to financial management and clinical development, we'll provide actionable advice and strategies for building a dental practice that not only delivers top-quality care to patients, but also generates long-term financial stability and success. Whether you're just starting out in the field or are looking to take your existing practice to the next level, Dentistry Made Simple has something for you.

https://Stitcher.com/show/tbone-speaks-dental-podcast

Dentistry Uncensored

Hosted by Dr. Howard Farran & powered by Dentaltown

dentaltown

Uncomplicate your dental life with Dr. Howard Farran as he interviews your fellow townies and leaders in dentistry. Dentists and dental professionals share their wisdom to make your dentistry faster, easier, higher in quality and lower in cost. Episodes released every weekday with the full transcripts at:

Dentaltown.com/podcasts

Dentists, Implants and Worms

Hosted by Dr Justin Moody & Dr. Randy Houska

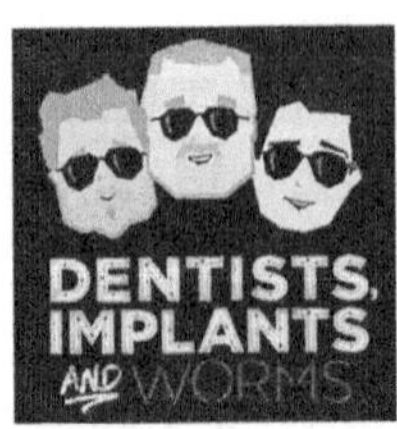

Helping you navigate the world of dentistry - one vodka-soda at a time! This is not your average dental podcast. Join Dr. Justin Moody and Dr. Randy Houska along with a variety of other personalities. Dr. Justin Moody invites dozens upon dozens of his colleagues, mentors and inspirations in the world of dentistry who he interviews in a real and unfiltered format. It's just good, honest conversation and a whole lot of Fireball.

http://DentistsImplantsAndWorms.com

Dentistry's Growing

Hosted by Grace Rizza

Dental Marketing Leader, Grace Rizza hosts Dentistry's Growing with Grace, a dental podcast about marketing, entrepreneurship, and leadership. Get the industry's top innovation, tips, and advice while enjoying a moment of positivity.

https://GraceRizza.com/podcast/

DNA Podcast

Hosted by Kira Dineen

PEOPLE'S CHOICE
PODCAST AWARD
WINNER

Discover new advances in the world of genetics. Winner of "Best 2020 and 2021 Science and Medicine Podcast Awards", the show educates on genetic and public health topics through event coverage, news stories, book/movie reviews, and interviews. Guests include genetic counselors, researchers, patient advocates and professors in the field of genetics.

https://DNAPodcast.com/

Doctor Entrepreneur Podcast

Hosted by Glenn Vo

If you are a Healthcare Professional that wants to grow their business or make an impact beyond the four walls of your practice, then this is the podcast for you. Dr. Glenn Vo interviews entrepreneurs and industry leaders to not only share their stories but to share their pearls of wisdom to get you inspired and empowered.

https://podcasts.apple.com/us/podcast/doctor-entrepreneur-podcast/id1479036670

Elevate Orthodontics

Hosted by Dr. Lance Miller

This show connects orthodontists with guests who can provide tangible increases in knowledge, judgment and clinical acumen. You'll hear motivational and inspirational empowerment to enable a proactive style of personal leadership and management recognizing the critical importance of "soft skills" while not forgetting the logistical and details that lead to success.

https://ElevateOrthopodcast.com/

Extracting Wisdom

Hosted by Brandon Evert

Prevent the decay of YOUR future by Extracting Wisdom with Brandon Evert! Discover what life is like as a pre-dental student and learn Brandon's proven strategies for successful dental school admission. Follow him throughout his dental school years as he documents the journey towards his dream career in dentistry. He hopes to create an enthusiastic community of future dentists that will rock the world of dentistry!

https://podcasts.apple.com/us/podcast/extracting-wisdom/id1347733635

Hygiene Superstar

Hosted by Dr Mike Czubiak and Dr Tom Larkin

Dental Hygienists and prevented minded dentists are the real heroes in the fight against chronic inflammatory diseases. Dr. Mike Czubiak and Dr. Tom Larkin explore the mouth-body connection and talk about implementable strategies that will help your patients live a happier, healthier life.

https://HygieneSuperstar.com/podcast/

Kevin Speaks Dental

Hosted by Kevin Henry

This podcast is about finding YOU, understanding YOU, unapologetically being YOU, and actively going after your personal and professional goals. The podcast features interviews and stories that are designed to educate and inspire. Every episode dives deep into compelling stories that need to be heard. From diversity and inclusion to mental health and everything in between Kevin P. Henry will be the guide for greater learning and awareness.

https://KevinSpeaksDental.com/

Life and Dentistry

Hosted by Dr. Cole Hackett and Joe Blalock

Helpful insight, honest guidance, and witty banter about the dentist's journey. Whether you're in dental school, recently graduated, hunting for an associateship, or thinking about starting your own practice – pull up a seat. The Life & Dentistry Podcast was created to serve as a round table for dental professionals to come together, share laughs, and lift one another up. They go beyond being an educational resource and aim to also provide a valuable community where dentists can all learn from each other and find that balance between life and work that made you choose dentistry in the first place!

https://LifeAndDentistry.com/

Mommy Dentists in Business

Hosted by Dr Grace Yum, DDS

Dr. Grace Yum has quietly become one of the highest profile pediatric dentists in Chicago and beyond. She is certified in pediatrics and has founded and built Yummy Dental and Orthodontics for Kids into a leader in its category. In her podcasts, Dr. Yum shares pearls of wisdom based on her experience that are designed to help moms be successful in their medical careers and in their lives more broadly. She interviews a rotating cast of experts who give invaluable advice from a variety of perspectives: lawyers, CEOs, nutritionists, parenting experts and more. Along the way, Dr. Yum shares the secrets to her success in balancing motherhood and her growing business interests in dental, real estate and beyond.

https://MommyDibs.com/podcast/

New Dentists on the Block

Hosted by Dr. Tonya Sue Maistas

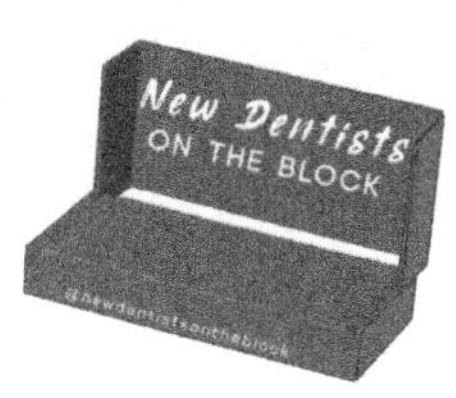

Navigating dentistry can be challenging. That's why Tonya Sue Dr. Maistas is committed to helping new dentists learn how to succeed and thrive in their dental practice. She interviews top docs who share their stories, experiences, and challenges in life as well as in the office.

Zencastr.com/New-Dentists-on-the-block

Nifty Thrifty Dentists

Hosted by Dr. Glenn Vo and Dr. Vinh Nguyen

NIFTY Thrifty Dentists

Dr. Glenn Vo and Dr. Vinh Nguyen are the original "Odd Couple" of Dentistry - they are neither partners in practice or in bed. Just the dynamic duo behind one of the most entertaining dental podcasts out there. Let's face it. Being a dental professional is hard. Heck, life in general is hard. Leave reality for a moment and join us in this podcast whirlwind of interesting guests, funny jokes, and thought-provoking banter.

https://NiftyThriftyDentists.com/podcast/

Nobody Told Me

Hosted by Teresa Duncan

Insurance expert Teresa Duncan explores the dental business from behind-the-scenes of the industry to tackle important management and business issues in the office. Frequent co-host, Keven Henry throws in his viewpoint, so you won't ever be in the position where you find yourself saying, "Nobody told me that."

https://NobodyToldMeThat.libsyn.com

Peaceful Practice

Hosted by Dr. Alan Mead and Dr. Dawn Kulongowski

The Peaceful Practice Podcast delivers real life conversations for stressed out professionals. Dr. Alan Mead and Dr. Dawn Kulongowski share a unique and honest perspective on stress management honestly and with a heavy dose of humor. They discuss both the stress and the strategies for dealing with the stress of juggling life, family, and practice management bringing the wisdom of meditation and mindfulness teachings to professionals and their practices.

https://PeacefulPractice.com/podcast/

Prosperident's Dental Practice Owner's Podcast

Hosted by David Harris

Protect yourself from fraud and embezzlement. Prosperident is the world's oldest and largest firm providing dental embezzlement investigation and embezzlement protection services to general dentists and dental specialists. This podcast is chock-full of tools, strategies, and tips to help run your practice better.

https://Prosperident.com/prosperident-podcasts/

Protrusion Dental Podcast

Hosted by Jaz Gulati

From the UK comes The Protrusive Dental Podcast. The entertaining Jaz Gulati discusses hot topics in dentistry including occlusion, working abroad, course reviews, clinical tips and personal development strategies to add value to your life and career.

https://Protrusive.co.uk/

Relentless Dentist

Hosted by Dr. David Maloley

Elevating confidence, culture, and cash flow for single-location dental practice owners, Dr. Dave utilizes over a decade of practice ownership and consulting experience to help dentists grow their take-home pay while spending less time at the office. He's the author of "Dentist on a Mission" and speaks at many of dentistry's top meetings.

https://RelentlessDentist.com/

Tale of Two Hygienists

Hosted by https://www.ataleoftwohygienists.com/

Produced by two dental hygienists with over 20 years combined experience, A Tale of Two Hygienists launched in 2015 to help hygienists provide better care for their patients while promoting the joys of being a dental hygienist.

https://ATaleOfTwoHygienists.com/

Talking Nachos

Hosted by Dr. Paul "Nacho" Goodman

Paul "Dr. Nacho" Goodman is founder of the 20k+ member Facebook group, Dental Nachos. A dentist, dad, and husband Dr. Nacho shares golden nacho tips to help you survive and thrive in the real world of dentistry. Developing your dentist core and strengthening your mind, words and hand skills is the key to being a successful dentist and decreasing the number of times you feel like crying on the inside part of your body each day.

https://DentalNachos.com

Talking with the Toothcop

Hosted by Duane "Tink" Tinker

Duane Tinker used to investigate 'naughty' dentists as a state police investigator for the Texas Dental Board. He traded in his badge and gun for opportunity and a chance to share his knowledge and experience with dentists trying to do the right thing. He recognized that most dentists and their staff care about doing the right thing. With the multitude of rules and regulations there is large gap between what they know and what they should know. Tink believed he could make a difference with his knowledge and experience to make dental offices safer for patients, dentists and their dental teams. Tink and his team have supported nearly 900 clients and over 1500 dental offices.

https://dentalcompliance.com/pages/podcast-1

The Authentic Dentist

Hosted by Dr. Allison House & Shawn Zajas

At the core of the authentic dentist is the belief that the answer to the current challenges in dentistry, is dentists discovering that your greatest asset and point of differentiation is your personal brand. Dr. Allison House of House Dental in Scottsdale, AZ and Shawn Zajas, founder of Zana, help you extend your care beyond the chair and take you deeper down the journey of authenticity to reach greater fulfillment in your professional lives while delivering remarkable experiences to the patients you serve.

https://podcasts.apple.com/us/podcast/the-authentic-dentist/id1487586274

The Best Practices Show

Hosted by Kirk Behrendt

Learn the SECRETS of the best dental practices with Kirk Behrendt, CEO of ACT Dental, through interviews with leaders in the industry. Kirk Behrendt is the Founder of ACT Dental, a customized coaching company for dentists. He has invested his entire professional life studying the top dental practices in the world and the leadership that guides them.

https://The-Best-Practices-Show.captivate.fm/listen

The Dental Amigos

Hosted by Rob Montgomery and Dr. Paul Goodman

Dentistry can be a lonely profession without good friends. The Dental Amigos hope to serve as a resource for dentists and those who like, love or spend time with dentists, and to bring the dental world together for the RIGHT reasons–fun, friendship and (practical) learning inside and outside of the operatory.

https://TheDentalAmigos.com/podcast-archive/

The Dental Business

Hosted by Amir Moghaddam and Ardi Safi

ACTdental

This dental-specific podcast that hosts industry leaders to discuss hot topics in the dental field. The goal is to share creative ideas to grow your dental practice, debunk some dental myths, discuss leading tech used in the industry, and even financial management. Every Friday the show also has a "Marketing Fridays" episode that covers marketing-specific topics hosted by Amir and Ardi the founders of DDS Marketing.

Topics covered include:

- Can you double your revenue in 6 months?
- How to get more high-ticket patients
- Are you ready for a second location?
- What are the opportunities during a recession?
- Should I focus on specialty or bread-and-butter dentistry?
- How to leverage your influence to grow your practice

Tune in every Wednesday and Friday for a new episode.

https://open.spotify.com/show/0RkYzEpPOTnVH9Vid4GGlE?si=JEA3QPeZThCGnNDKKiWJmw

The Dental Experience

Hosted by Ryan Vet

No matter your role, as dental professionals, it is our responsibility to provide exemplary patient experience and care. In each episode of this dental podcast, you will hear from experts on how to create a positive patient experience while simultaneously growing your practice. Hosted by Ryan Vet, dental speaker, author and entrepreneur, this is your one-stop for everything you need to know to have a thriving dental practice and a fulfilled life.

https://TheDentalPodcast.com/

The Dental Marketer

Hosted by Michael Arias

Looking to attract more patients to your practice? This podcast answers your core dental marketing questions and concerns breaking down campaigns and strategies. Host Michael Arias talks all about Ground Marketing and has an inspiring style that is sure to motivate to take the actions you need to succeed

https://TheDentalMarketer.site/podcast

The Dental Practice Fixers

Hosted by Dr. Richard H. Madow

The Madow Center
for DENTAL PRACTICE SUCCESS

For thirty years Dr. Richard Madow has been helping dentists reach levels of success they never before imagined. Through his inspirational speaking, coaching, new patient programs, and much more, Dr. Madow is known as a key opinion leader in the profession. As one of the founders of The Best Seminar Ever, Dr. Madow is no stranger to motivating docs and team members to great success and happiness.

https://Madow.com/dental-practice-fixers-podcast/

The Dental Practice Heroes

Hosted by Dr. Paul Etchison

This dental business podcast is full of in-depth discussions and meaningful strategies that you can implement your very next workday. All content is intended to be practical for dentists, and applicable to anyone working in the dental field including doctors, hygienists, dental assistants, and admin personnel.

https://DentalPracticeHeroes.com/

The Dentalpreneur Podcast

Hosted by Dr. Mark Costes

The Dentalpreneur Podcast is one of the most listened to dental podcasts in the country. This isn't your typical dental podcast. With tens of thousands of listeners each month, Mark provides his listeners with topics ranging from business, marketing, services, motivational and entertaining. Plus, Mark interviews big names outside the dental world including astronaut Clayton Anderson, athlete Ben Greenfield, author Ryan Holiday and more!

https://TrueDentalSuccess.com/the-dentalpreneur-podcast/

The 8E8 Show

Hosted by Joshua Scott

The 8E8 (pronounced "88") Show is an entertaining and informative podcast answering dentistry's most important marketing questions. Hosted by Joshua Scott, this podcast explores a myriad of strategies to help you attract more patients and grow the profitability of your practice.

https://JoshuaScott.com/video-type/8e8-show

The Raving Patients Podcast

Hosted by Dr. Len Tau

On The Raving Patients Podcast, Dr Len Tau (known as the "Reviews Doctor") offers creative strategies and real-world tactics on growing a dental practice. He has taken the tools that he has learned over the 23 years as a practicing dentist and shares them along with his guests' tips with his audience. Topics discussed range from online reputation marketing, social media, and case acceptance to how to increase production and collections. His weekly podcast is a "must" listen for anyone looking to grow their practice. Listeners learn not only how to revitalize their practice's online reputation but also how to increase their visibility and credibility on Google.

http://RavingPatientsPodcast.com/

The Shared Practices Podcast

Hosted by Dr. Richard Low and Dr. George Hariri

With years of topics and segments that span from how to purchase your first practice to understanding the day-to-day operations of your business, Shared Practices takes the mystery out of practice ownership and puts the information directly in your hands. Sure to entertain, this show delivers relevant conversations with visionaries, clinicians and your friends in the dental space.

https://SharedPractices.com/podcasts/shared-practices

The Tooth Sleuth Podcast

Hosted by Greg Essenmacher

The Tooth Sleuth podcast is hosted by Greg Essenmacher who is committed to "Helping Dentists and Dental Professionals Maximize Their Potential". From vision to execution, Greg talks with this generation's leading figures in the dental field having interesting conversations and creating business strategies that work.

https://podcasts.apple.com/us/podcast/the-tooth-sleuth-podcast/id1582735598

Tooth or Dare

Hosted by Hygienist Irene Michelle Iancu

Hold on to your suction, it's about to get viscous. If you are looking for a fun, hip and happening podcast, Irene will keep you entertained with her stories about her dental hygienist career, practice ownership, social media and, of course, dental-related content. On Tooth or Dare, she gives mic-dropping solutions to your dental questions and problems as a dental professional. This show has something for everyone interested in oral health and personal and professional development.

https://Linktr.ee/toothordare.podcast

Totally Oral

Hosted by Dr. Russell Schafer & Dr. Clinton Scott Timmerman

Much like Seinfeld, Totally Oral is a dental podcast about "nothing". It simply exists. Brought to you from the big easy in New Orleans and the Rocky Mountains of Colorado, Drs. Russell Schafer and Clinton Scott Timmerman have fun and entertaining conversation about real-life dentistry experiences. If you like geeking out and hearing the latest and greatest directly from the doctor's mouth, listen in and laugh with these two amusing docs.

https://TotallyOral.Libsyn.com

Very Dental Podcast Network

Hosted by Dr. Gary DeWood

verydental PODCAST NETWORK With over ten years of dental podcast expertise, renowned host Dr. Alan Mead has over 4.3 million downloads of his informative and entertaining dental podcasts. The Very Dental Podcast continues Dr. Mead's legacy he built by co-leading The Dental Hacks podcast. Dr. Mead is still hosting the best guests in the industry to come on the show and share their expertise. So, tune in, turn up, and learn a thing or two about all things dental.

https://VeryDentalPodcast.com/

VIP Smiles

Hosted by Catrise Austin

Known to many as The Queen of Smiles™ and Cosmetic Dentist to the stars, Dr. Catrise Austin shares some of the best oral health tips on a variety of topics including teeth whitening, porcelain veneers, smile makeovers, and more. Voted as one of the "Top 25 Women In Dentistry" by Dental Products Report Magazine and also named as one of Kleer's "Most Influential Dentist's in America", Dr. Austin is an award-winning cosmetics dentist who has an A-list of famous celebrities including Cardi B, DJ Khaled, Wendy Williams, Anthony Anderson, and Common to name a few.

https://VipSmiles.com/lets-talk-smiles-podcast/

Voices from The Bench

Hosted by Dr. Elvis Dahl and Barbara Warner Wojdan

A weekly podcast dedicated to the dental laboratory industry. Featuring anyone associated with the profession from all over the world. Your hosts are actively involved with dental laboratories helping beautiful smiles and interviewing people from the industry on their time off. New episodes every Monday morning.

https://VoicesFromTheBench.com/

What the Hell Just Happened?

Hosted by CEDR CEO Paul Edwards

HR Challenges are real. For over 40 years, Paul Edwards has been managing employees and growing businesses. In this informative podcast, Paul gives you the lowdown to protect your practice and shares real world HR horror stories that will make you laugh, cringe, and cry. Learn how to navigate the stinky staff, nursing mothers, sexual misconduct, and all the other crazy workplace issues that make you ask, "What the hell just happened?"

https://CEDRSolutions.com/podcast

Working Interferences Dental Podcast

Hosted by Drs. Joshua Austin DDS and Lance Timmerman DMD

A dental podcast for the AVERAGE dentist. No question is too controversial for Joshua Austin DDS and Lance Timmerman DMD. Questions are NOT "best bonding agent" or "best impression material," these questions are the ones that are burning desire types. You know, like "can I harm my assistant for being annoying?", or "how much oral sex is too much after gum grafts?

https://WorkingInterferences.podbean.com/

Yoga for Dentists

Hosted by Dr. Josie Dovidio

Yoga for Dentists is a podcast for wellness-minded dental professionals. Host Dr. Josie Dovidio has been a general dentist since 1997 and is also a registered yoga teacher and certified wellness consultant.

She offers wellness and mindset tips and guided meditations designed specifically for dental professionals. She also interviews dental industry leaders as well as experts in the health and wellness field, about setting dental professionals up for success and longevity in both their careers and their lives!

https://yogafordentists.net/podcast/

Made in the USA
Coppell, TX
22 February 2023

13275139R00177